FACES
OF
THE
ENEMY

Sam Keen

FACES OF THE ENEMY

Reflections of the Hostile Imagination

Photo Editor Anne Page

1817

Harper & Row, Publishers, San Francisco
Cambridge, Hagerstown, New York, Philadelphia
London, Mexico City, São Paulo, Singapore, Sydney

Other Books by Sam Keen

Beginnings Without End
Apology For Wonder
To A Dancing God
Voices and Visions
The Passionate Life
Gabriel Marcel
What to Do When You're Bored and Blue
Telling Your Story with Ann Valley Fox
Life Maps with Jim Fowler

Library of Congress Cataloging-in-Publication Data

Keen, Sam.
　　Faces of the enemy.

　　Bibliography: p. (TC?)
　　1. Hostility (Psychology) 2. War—Psychological
aspects. 3. Propaganda—Psychological aspects.
4. Projection (Psychology) 5. Paranoia. I. Title.
BF575.H6K44 1986　　303.6′6　　85-45358
ISBN 0–06–250471–1

FIRST EDITION

Design: Design Office, Peter Martin

86 87 88 89 90 RRD 10 9 8 7 6 5 4 3 2 1

CONTENTS

For the new breed of heroes and heroines who dare to struggle with the enemy within and look at the shadow of evil that obscures every human heart.

In the hope that by disarming the self we may find the clarity to envision and the courage to create a new social order free of organized carnage and sanctified genocide.

For our children, especially Lael, Gifford, Jessamyn, who teach us time and time again that love can triumph over enmity.

To Create an Enemy

Start with an empty canvas
Sketch in broad outline the forms of
men, women, and children.

Dip into the unconscious well of your own
disowned darkness
with a wide brush and
stain the strangers with the sinister hue
of the shadow.

Trace onto the face of the enemy the greed,
hatred, carelessness you dare not claim as
your own.

Obscure the sweet individuality of each face.

Erase all hints of the myriad loves, hopes,
fears that play through the kaleidoscope of
every finite heart.

Twist the smile until it forms the downward
arc of cruelty.

Strip flesh from bone until only the
abstract skeleton of death remains.

Exaggerate each feature until man is
metamorphasized into beast, vermin, insect.

Fill in the background with malignant
figures from ancient nightmares—devils,
demons, myrmidons of evil.

When your icon of the enemy is complete
you will be able to kill without guilt,
slaughter without shame.

The thing you destroy will have become
merely an enemy of God, an impediment
to the sacred dialectic of history.

INTRODUCTION

Homo Hostilis, The Enemy Maker

Since wars begin in the minds of men,
it is in the minds of men
that we have to erect the ramparts of peace.

UNESCO Charter

Jerry Robinson
© 1985 by Cartoonists and Writers Syndicate

In the beginning we create the enemy. Before the weapon comes the image. We *think* others to death and then invent the battle-axe or the ballistic missiles with which to actually kill them. Propaganda precedes technology.

Politicians of both the left and right keep getting things backward. They assume the enemy will vanish if only we manage our weapons differently. Conservatives believe the enemy will be frightened into civility if we have bigger and better weapons. Liberals believe the enemy will become our friend if we have smaller and fewer weapons. Both proceed from rationalistic, optimistic assumptions: we human beings are reasonable, pragmatic, tool-making animals. We have progressed thus far in history by becoming *Homo sapiens* ("rational human") and *Homo faber* ("tool-making human"). Therefore, we can make peace by rational negotiation and arms control.

But it isn't working. The problem seems to lie not in our reason or our technology, but in the hardness of our hearts. Generation after generation, we find excuses to hate and dehumanize each other, and we always justify ourselves with the most mature-sounding political rhetoric. And we refuse to admit the obvious. We human beings are *Homo hostilis*, the hostile species, the enemy-making animal. We are driven to fabricate an enemy as a scapegoat to bear the burden of our denied enmity. From the unconscious residue of our hostility, we create a target; from our private demons, we conjure a public enemy. And, perhaps, more than anything else, the wars we engage in are compulsive rituals, shadow dramas in which we continually try to kill those parts of ourselves we deny and despise.

Our best hope for survival is to change the way we think about enemies and warfare. Instead of being hypnotized by the enemy we need to begin looking at the eyes with which we see the enemy. Now it is time to explore the mind of *Homo hostilis* ("hostile human"), we need to examine in detail how we manufacture the image of the enemy, how we create surplus evil, how we turn the world into a killing ground. It seems unlikely that we will have any considerable success in controlling warfare unless we come to understand the logic of political paranoia, and the process of creating propaganda that justifies our hostility. We need to become conscious of what Carl Jung called "the shadow." The heroes and leaders toward peace in our time will be those men and women who have the courage to plunge into the darkness at the bottom of the personal and the corporate psyche and face the enemy within. Depth psychology has presented us with the undeniable wisdom that the enemy is constructed from denied aspects of the self. Therefore, the radical commandment "Love your enemy as yourself" points the way toward both self-knowledge and peace. We do, in fact, love or hate our enemies to the same degree that we love or hate ourselves. In the image of the enemy, we will find the mirror in which we may see our own face most clearly.

But wait a minute. Not so fast! A chorus of objections arises from the practitioners of realistic power politics: "What do you mean, 'create' enemies? We don't make enemies. There are aggressors, evil empires, bad men, and wicked women in the real world. And they will destroy us if we don't destroy them first. There are real villains—Hitler, Stalin, Pol Pot (leader of the Cambodian Khmer Rouge, responsible for the murder of 2 million of his own people). You can't psychologize political events, or solve the problem of war by studying perceptions of the enemy."

Objections sustained. In part. Half-truths of a psychological or political nature are not apt to advance the cause of peace. We should be as wary of psychologizing political events as we should be of politicizing psychological events. War is a complex problem that is not likely to be solved by any single approach or discipline.

11

To deal with it we need, at the very minimum, a *quantum* theory of warfare rather than a single-cause theory. As we understand light only by considering it as both particle and wave, we will get leverage on the problem of war only by seeing it as a system that is sustained by both:

The warrior psyche	and	The violent polis
Paranoia	and	Propaganda
The hostile imagination	and	Value and geopolitical conflicts between nations

Creative thinking about war will always involve considering both the individual psyche and social institutions. Society shapes the psyche and vice versa. Therefore, we have to work at the tasks of creating psychological and political alternatives to war, changing the psyche of *Homo hostilis* and the structure of international relations. Both a heroic journey into the self and a new form of compassionate politics. We have no chance of lessening warfare unless we look at the psychological roots of paranoia, projection, and propaganda, nor if we ignore the harsh child-rearing practices, the injustice, the special interests of the power elites, the historic racial, economic, and religious conflicts and population pressures that sustain the war system.

The primary task of this book is to fill a void in our thinking about war. Look in any library and you will find books that deal with every imaginable aspect of war except one—the enemy. One would suppose that, since war is designed to kill the enemy, someone would have thought long and hard about the identity of the enemy. Those assigned to kill him—the military—usually leave the task of defining who the enemy is, and why he must be destroyed, to politicians. The military prefer the limited role of training men to kill, dealing with means, tactics, and strategy. Ordinarily, the job of turning civilians into soldiers involves a liberal use of propaganda and hate training. A variety of dehumanizing faces is superimposed over the enemy to allow him to be killed without guilt. The problem in military psychology is how to convert the act of murder into patriotism. For the most part, this process of dehumanizing the enemy has not been closely examined. When we project our shadows, we systematically blind ourselves to what we are doing. To mass produce hatred, the body politic must remain unconscious of its own paranoia, projection, and propaganda. "The enemy" is thus considered as real and objective as a rock or a mad dog. So our first task is to break this taboo, make conscious the unconscious of the body politic, and examine the ways in which we create an enemy.

To do this, I will construct in Part 1 what philosophers call a "phenomenology of the hostile imagination." This task requires that I bracket the historical question of guilt and innocence, and focus on the recurring images that have been used in different times and places to characterize the enemy. My initial quest is for what Jung would have called "the archetype" of the enemy. What we will find is that wars come and go, but—strangely, amid changing circumstances—the hostile imagination has a certain standard repertoire of images it uses to dehumanize the enemy. In matters of propaganda, we are all platonists; we apply eternal archetypes to changing events.

Needless to say, in certain circumstances, such as the war against the Third Reich, the images we hold of the enemy seem almost realistic. Hitler was such a perfect devil incarnate, a paragon of evil, that we have been using him ever since to vilify our enemies. Just because the paranoid mind projects its rejected vices onto the enemy does *not* automatically mean the enemy is innocent of these projections. As popular wisdom tells us, paranoids sometimes have real enemies. Nevertheless, we can never determine our own degree of complicity in the creation of evil unless we are willing, for a moment, to suspend our belief in all propaganda and study the sources of the projections of the hostile imagination. After we have been willing to look honestly at the eyes with which we see the enemy, we will still be left with the agonizing decision of when we should take up arms to resist a particular enemy. Studying the psychology of perception, the logic of *Homo hostilis* will not eliminate conflict, but it may make us examine our own motives and will introduce a healthy doubt into our otherwise self-righteous conduct of warfare.

After we have examined the archetypes of the enemy, we will, in Part 2, turn the spotlight within and look at some of the psychological roots of the habit of enmity, and how we may reclaim the shadow we have projected onto the enemy.

In the final part of the book, we will look at a variety of scenarios for the future of enmity. Here we will move from the most minimal political possibilities to the most radical psychological option, from the desperate hope that we may die with dignity in the nuclear apocalypse to the near-utopian hope that we may find political and psychological equivalents of war and create a new human being—*Homo amicus* ("friendly human")—who is animated by kindness, has a friendly psyche, and a politics of compassion.

PART 1

ARCHETYPES OF THE ENEMY

Apparitions of the Hostile Imagination

Look carefully at the face of the enemy. The lips are curled downward. The eyes are fanatical and far away. The flesh is contorted and molded into the shape of monster or beast. Nothing suggests this man ever laughs, is torn by doubts, or shaken by tears. He feels no tenderness or pain. Clearly he is unlike us. We need have no sympathy, no guilt, when we destroy him.

In all propaganda, the face of the enemy is designed to provide a focus for our hatred. He is the other. The outsider. The alien. He is not human. If we can only kill him, we will be rid of all within and without ourselves that is evil.

How are these faces of the enemy created? And why is the repertoire of images so universal?

THE ENEMY AS STRANGER

Consensual Paranoia

No one knows for certain when warfare became an abiding human habit. Some archaeologists believe there was a pre-Neolithic Eden peopled by peaceful hunters and gatherers, and that greed and systematic violence arose only when the agricultural revolution created sufficient surplus wealth to tempt some men to steal what others had produced. The best evidence we have suggests that warfare is no more than 13,000 years old. According to Sue Mansfield, our earliest human artifacts from the Paleolithic period testify to hunting, art, myth, and ritual, but give no pictures of men engaged in battle.[1]

Once invented, warfare became a nearly universal practice. But there are enough exceptions to establish the crucial point on which hope rests its delicate case: enemy making and warfare are social creations rather than biological imperatives. The peaceful peoples, such as the Hopi, the Tasaday, the Mbuti Pygmies, the K'ung Bushmen of the Kalahari, the Copper Eskimo, the Amish, and others, show us that human beings are capable of creating sophisticated cultures without the use of systematic violence, without a warrior class and a

Bolshevism, the Killer of Germany
Germany, W.W.II

The Tokyo Kid
U.S., W.W. II

psyche organized around defending the tribe against an enemy. According to Geoffrey Gorer,

> The most significant common traits in these peaceful societies are that they all manifest enormous gusto for concrete physical pleasures—eating, drinking, sex, laughter—and that they all make very little distinction between the ideal characters of men and women, particularly that they have no ideal of brave, aggressive masculinity. . . . They do not have heroes or martyrs to emulate or cowards or traitors to despise; their religious life lacks significant personalized gods and devils; a happy, hardworking and productive life is within the reach of all.[2]

The parable of the gentle tribes teaches us that there is nothing in our genes or in the essential human condition that makes warfare an inevitable human destiny. Moreover, says Ashley Montagu,

> Throughout the two million years of man's evolution the highest premium has been placed on cooperation, not merely intragroup cooperation, but also intergroup cooperation, or else there would be no human beings today.[3]

For the moment, let us note this thread of hope as we turn to the study of the more common human condition of consensual paranoia and the world created by the hostile imagination. In times past and present (and, we hope, future), there have existed people governed more by the spirit of Eros than the dark hand of Thanatos.

Sadly, the majority of tribes and nations create a sense of social solidarity and membership in part by systematically creating enemies. The corporate identity of most peoples depends on dividing the world into a basic antagonism:

Us	versus	Them
Insiders	versus	Outsiders
The tribe	versus	The enemy

In other words, paranoia, far from being an occasional individual pathology is the normal human condition. It is considered both normal and admirable, the essence of tribal loyalty and patriotism, to direct vitriolic hatred toward strangers we hardly know, and to reserve love for those familiar to us. The habit of directing our hostility outward toward those who are unknown to us

17

is as characteristic of human beings as our capacity for reason, wonder, or tool making. In fact, it is most often *Homo hostilis* who directs the energies of *Homo sapiens* and *Homo faber.* Our hostility regularly perverts reason into rationalization and propaganda, and makes our creativity serve the forces of destruction by making swords rather than plowshares.

The hostile imagination begins with a simple but crippling assumption: what is strange or unknown is dangerous and intends us evil. The unknown is untrustworthy. The Latin word *hostis* originally meant a stranger, one not connected to us by kin or ties of blood.

Around the basic antagonism between insiders and strangers the tribal mind forms an entire myth of conflict. The mythic mind, which still governs modern politics, is obsessively dualistic. It splits everything into polar opposites. The basic distinction between insiders and outsiders is parlayed into a paranoid ethic and metaphysic in which reality is seen as a morality play, a conflict between

The tribes	versus	The enemy
Good	versus	Evil
The Sacred	versus	The profane

One primary function of this paranoid metaphysic of *Homo hostilis* is to justify the killing of outsiders and to rationalize warfare. Myth, besides telling us who we are, where we came from, and what is our destiny,

Love adds and multiplies.
Hate divides and subtracts.
Sandor McNab

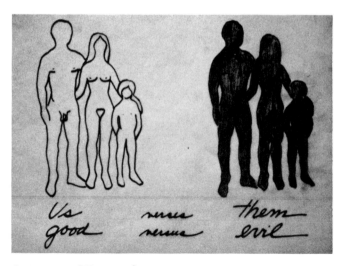

Consensual Paranoia
Jeanette Stobie

sanctions the killing of strangers who are considered nonhuman and profane. Myth makes killing or dying in war a sacred act performed in the service of some god or immortal ideal. Thus, the creation of propaganda is as old as the hostile imagination. Truth is the first sacrifice we make in order to belong to any exclusive group.

THE ENEMY AS AGGRESSOR

The Logic of Paranoia

Arafat as Shadow
De La Torre. Columbia
© 1985 by Cartoonists and Writers Syndicate

Consensual paranoia—the pathology of the normal person who is a member of a war-justifying society—forms the template from which all the images of the enemy are created. By studying the logic of paranoia, we can see why certain archetypes of the enemy must necessarily recur, no matter what the historical circumstances.

Paranoia involves a complex of mental, emotional, and social mechanisms by which a person or a people claim righteousness and purity, and attribute hostility and evil to the enemy. The process begins with a splitting of the "good" self, with which we consciously identify and which is celebrated by myth and media, from the "bad" self, which remains unconscious so long as it may be projected onto an enemy. By this sleight of hand, the unacceptable parts of the self—its greed, cruelty, sadism, hostility, what Jung called "the shadow"—are made to disappear and are recognized only as qualities of the enemy. Paranoia reduces anxiety and guilt by transferring to the other all the characteristics one does not want to recognize in oneself. It is maintained by selective perception and recall. We only see and acknowledge those negative aspects of the enemy that support the stereotype we have already created. Thus, American television mainly reports bad news about the Russians, and vice versa. We remember only the evidence that confirms our prejudice.

As a metaphysic of threat, paranoia eliminates in advance any evidence that might contradict its basic assumption about the malevolent intent of the enemy. Hence, it makes it impossible to discriminate between realistic and purely imaginative dangers. A paranoid individual watching a man casually leaning against a building smoking a cigarette "knows" with absolute certainty that the man is signaling to another man in a window on the third floor of a building across the

I may sound a bit paranoid to you, but people just don't understand the threat.
Caspar Weinberger, 2/8/83

street, who in turn is in radio communication with the pilot of a plane flying overhead, who is about to zap our paranoid with invisible rays from a deadly laser gun. No amount of evidence will convince the paranoid mind that the assassination of President Kennedy was not an elaborate plot involving a network of sinister agents. Do the Russians seem to want peace? To the paranoid mind, this appearance is only further evidence that they are out to get us to disarm so they can conquer us. The double bind always built into paranoia makes its refutation logically impossible.

Nowhere is the paranoid mode better illustrated than in anti-Semitic propaganda. For the anti-Semite, the Jew is the fountainhead of evil. In back of the accidental, historical enemies of Germany—England, America, Russia—lurked the conspiratorial Jew. The threat was single and hidden to the casual eye, but obvious to the true believer in Aryan supremacy. Within this twisted logic, it made perfect sense for the Nazis to divert trains badly needed to transport troops to the front lines to take Jews to concentration camps for the "final solution."

Shades of the same paranoid vision color right-wing American anticommunists and obsessional Soviet anticapitalists, both of whom attribute to their adversaries more power, cohesion, and conspiratorial success than either has. True believers in both camps consider the world a battleground in which all countries will eventually have to be included within the sphere of influence of either capitalism or communism.

A major function of the paranoid mind is to escape

"He rides you all"
Germany, W.W.II

The Jew as Metathreat
Oslo 1941

"The Communists have no conscience. They drive good people to the battlefield to die in their 'human sea' onslaughts."
Nationalist leaflet dropped over mainland China.

"They are threatening us"
Jack Jurden. Wilmington Evening Journal News

from guilt and responsibility and affix blame elsewhere. This inversion can go to terrible extremes. Recently in San Francisco, a man raped and brutally cut off the arms of a young woman. When caught, he defended himself in court by claiming that she was threatening him. The attribution of blame to the other shows us that paranoia is rooted in arrested psychological development. Family therapists have a rule of thumb that says, The degree to which people blame is the degree to which they are still developmentally stuck in their family of origin; i.e., are still children. To blame is to deny both one's responsibility and one's potency. Paranoia is the refuge of children and victims.

Blame produces blame. Hence the paranoid person or nation will create a shared delusional system, a *paranoia à deux*. The enemy system involves a process of two or more enemies dumping their (unconscious) psychological wastes in each others' back yards. All we despise in ourselves we attribute to them. And vice versa. Since this process of unconscious projection of the shadow is universal, enemies "need" each other to dispose of their accumulated, disowned, psychological toxins. We form a hate bond, an "adversarial symbiosis," an integrated system that guarantees that neither of us will be faced with our own shadow.

"They are threatening us"
U.S.S.R.

In the current U.S.S.R.–U.S. conflict, we require each other as group-transference targets. Clearly, Soviet propaganda picturing the United States as an abuser of civil rights is the pot calling the kettle black. And just as clearly, our tirades against Soviet state control and lack of individual property reflect an unconscious anger at the real loss of individual freedom under corporate capitalism, and our dependence on the government to care for us from womb to tomb, neither of which fits our frontier image of ourselves as rugged individualists. We officially see their dependence on the state as slavery, and yet we have embraced big government and galloping socialism, and obviously have deep dependency needs that do not fit in with our conscious image of ourselves as "Marlboro man." And when the Soviets see our freedom to produce profit and consume as a form of license, it is clear that they long for greater personal freedom. We see the Soviets as making the individual a mere means to the goals of the state. They see us as sanctifying the greed of powerful individuals at the cost of community, and allowing the profit of the few at the expense of the many. And so long as we trade insults, we are both saved from the embarrassing task of looking at the serious faults and cruelties of our own systems.

Inevitably the paranoid, infantile psyche sees the enemy as having some of the paradoxical qualities of the bad parent. The formula necessary to destroy the enemy with moral impunity always attributes near-omnipotent power and a degraded moral character to the enemy. The U.S. Defense Department, in characteristic paranoid style, regularly discovers some gap—bomber gap, tank gap, missile gap, spending gap—that shows the Soviets are more powerful than the United States and it simultaneously paints a portrait of the ruthless advance of atheistic communism. The Kremlin plays the same game.

What is impossible for the paranoid mind is the very notion of equality. A paranoid must be either sadistically superior and dominate others, or masochistically inferior and feel threatened by them. Adults may be equal to one another, may share responsibility for good and evil, but in the infantile world, the giant—the parent, the enemy—has the power and therefore is morally despicable for not eliminating the pain and evil for which he alone is responsible.

Homo hostilis is incurably dualistic, a moralistic Manichean:

We are innocent.	They are guilty.
We tell the truth— inform.	They lie— use propaganda.
We only defend ourselves.	They are aggressors.
We have a defense department.	They have a war department.
Our missiles and weapons are designed to deter.	Their weapons are designed for a first strike.

Notice the undertone beneath the self-justification in all propaganda is the whining voice of the child: "He did it to me first"; "I only hit him back."

According to a new political dictionary just published in Moscow, "aggression may be defined as an armed attack on a country with the aim of seizing its territory and subjugating it economically and politically. Examples of aggression are the United States' war against the Vietnamese people and Israel's actions against Arab States." The same dictionary goes on to define the Soviet threat as "an anti-Soviet propaganda myth about a danger allegedly menacing the capitalist countries and coming from the Soviet Union. This absurd allegation is circulated in order to justify the arms race which brings fabulous profits to the magnates of the military-industrialist complex.[4]

Soviet Lies
Carmack. Christian Science Monitor
©1950 TCSPS

Paranoids hate/love each other.

Behind the fierce façade, *Homo hostilis* is a victim, a passive-aggressive who is obsessed with power because he feels impotent, having given over to the enemy the power of initiation and aggression. He who projects the power and responsibility for doing evil onto the enemy loses the ability to take initiative, to act. War is always reactionary, a drama in which two or more parties, who feel themselves powerless to do anything except respond to the aggressive initiative of the other, seek to demonstrate their superior potency.

Paranoia creates a self-fulfilling prophecy, a vicious circle in which suspicion breeds suspicion, threat breeds counterthreat. Passive-aggressive victims bring on themselves the aggression they obsessively fear. In the degree that the other is perceived as enemy, we respond "appropriately" by preparing to defend ourselves, with preemptive strikes if necessary. They react in similar fashion. Paranoids begin with imagined enemies and end up with real ones as the cycle of reaction turns into a complex historical conflict. In *paranoia à deux* hostility becomes synergistic, enemies become hypnotized by each other and become locked in a prison of mirrors. Human consciousness, it seems, is able to create or to discover almost any reality it focuses on long enough. We make the world in the image of what fascinates and terrifies us.

THE FACELESS ENEMY

Dehumanizing Propaganda

The object of warfare is to destroy or kill the enemy. But who is this enemy? Almost all works on war refer to the enemy obliquely. A strange silence pervades political, military, and popular thought on this matter. Our reluctance to think clearly about the enemy appears to be an unconscious conspiracy. We systematically blur distinctions and insist that the enemy remain faceless, because we are able to perpetuate the horror of war, to be the authors of unthinkable suffering only when we blind ourselves to what we are doing. Traditionally we have maintained this practice of unthinking by creating dehumanizing stereotypes of the objects of our violence and reserving our rational thought for determining the weapons, strategies, and tactics we will use in destroying "them."

The Faceless Soviet
Oliphant, by Pat Oliphant. Copyright, 1982,
Universal Press Syndicate. Used by permission.
All rights reserved.

Laurens Van der Post recounts how one mechanism of dehumanization worked in a Japanese prison camp during World War II:

The Hun — his Mark
Blot it Out
with
LIBERTY BONDS

The Enemy as It
U.S., W.W.I

I was ordered to go in there and destroy the enemy. . . . I did not sit down and think in terms of men, women, and children. They were all classified the same, and that was the classification that we dealt with, just as enemy soldiers.
Lt. William Calley, Jr.

The Japanese showed a sudden reluctance to meet our eyes in the course of our daily contacts. We knew that they were taking precautions to ensure that not a single glimpse of one's obvious and defenseless humanity should slip through their defenses and contradict the caricature some demoniac *a priori* image had made of us within them. The nearer the storm came the more intense the working of this mechanism became. I had seen its most striking manifestation in the eyes of a Japanese officer who, with a condemned Ambonese soldier before him, had had to lean forward and brush the long black hair from the back of the neck over the head and eyes of the condemned man before he could draw his sword and cut off the man's head. Before the blow fell he had been compelled to look straight ahead over the doomed head seeing neither it nor us who stood, raggedly, in a long line in front of him.[5]

As a rule, human beings do not kill other human beings. Before we enter into warfare or genocide, we first dehumanize those we mean to "eliminate." Before the Japanese performed medical experiments on human guinea pigs in World War II, they named them *maruta* — logs of wood. The hostile imagination systematically destroys our natural tendency to identify with others of our species. *Homo hostilis* cripples imagination by forcing it to serve the limited purposes of hatred and propaganda. A full-bodied imagination would lead us to the recognition that those we are fighting against are like ourselves. They hurt when struck, fear death, love their children, hate going to war, and are filled with feelings of doubt and impotence.

The purpose of propaganda is to paralyze thought, to prevent discrimination, and to condition individuals to act as a mass. The modern warfare state removes the individuality of those who serve it by forcing them into uniform, and systematically destroys the complexities of those against whom it fights. "The" enemy is always singular, a limbolike category, to which we may assign any threat about which we do not wish to think clearly. The paranoid mind wraps the enemy in a fog. When war begins, clarity and charity are exiled for the duration. It is not a person we kill, but an idea. The art of propaganda is to create a portrait that incarnates the idea of what we wish to destroy so we will react rather than think, and automatically focus our free-floating

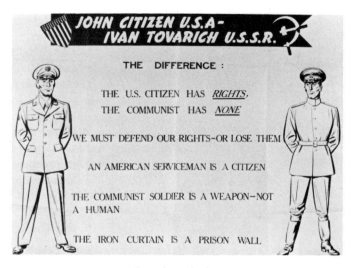

Cold War Black-White Simplistic Logic
U.S. Army

hostility, indistinct frustrations, and unnamed fears. The elements from which the portrait is assembled are standard curses and routine insults that have been in use since the beginning of recorded history.

When Western countries go to war against Asians, they usually portray them as faceless hordes. A U.S. Army film made during World War II characterized Japanese soldiers as "alike as photoprints from the same negative." We have habitually portrayed Asians as so different from ourselves that they place a low value on life. The old image of Genghis Khan and the Mongol hordes still haunts us and is retooled and pressed into service when needed. American forces in Korea found themselves swamped by an "ochre horde," a yellow tide of faceless masses, cruel and nerveless subhumans, the incomprehensible and the inscrutable Chinese, the human sea. Less than a generation later we were to face the same archtypically degraded enemy, now labeled "gooks," "dinks," "slopes," in Vietnam.

Front-line soldiers frequently report that when they come on an enemy dead and examine his personal effects—letters from home, pictures of loved ones—the propaganda image fades and it becomes difficult or impossible to kill again. Who can forget the moving scene in *All Quiet on the Western Front* when the German soldier is forced to spend the night in a foxhole with a Frenchman he has bayoneted?

THE ENEMY AS ENEMY OF GOD

War as Applied Theology

Martin Luther
Sixteenth-Century Woodcut

Therefore let everyone who can, smite, slay, and stab, secretly or openly, remembering that nothing can be more poisonous, hurtful, or devilish than a rebel. These are strange times when a prince can win heaven with bloodshed better than other men with prayer.
Martin Luther, 1525

The enemy is not merely flesh and blood but devil, demon, agent of the dark forces. Nor is warfare, ancient or modern, waged only on the historical field of battle. Behind the scenes of World War II, no less than in the Trojan Wars, competing gods directed the action of mortal warriors.

God and country may be quite separable in theory, but in day-to-day politics and religion they are fused. God santifies *our* social order, *our* way of life, *our* values, *our* territory. Thus, warfare is applied theology. Probe the rhetoric used to justify war, and you will find that every war is a "just" war, a crusade, a battle between the forces of good and evil. Warfare is a religio-political ritual in which the sacred blood of our heroes is sacrificed to hallow our ground and to destroy the enemies of God. Battle is the corporate ordeal through which the heroic nation justifies its claim, and refutes its enemies' claim, to be the chosen people of God, the bearers of an historical destiny, the representatives of the sacred.

That there is a seamless joining of religion and politics should be obvious from the way the rhetoric of warfare has been borrowed from theologians. Satan was regularly used by theologians and inquisitors to discredit their opponents. Catholic theologians said Luther's heresy should be dismissed because the voice of the devil was speaking through him. And Luther used the same rhetoric against the rebelling peasants, declaring them to be "the agents of the devil," and their revolt a prelude to the destruction of the world. He states as clearly as any other sacred warrior the terrible self-righteousness of holy war in which carnage becomes a devotion.

The most terrible of all the moral paradoxes, the Gordian knot that must be unraveled if history is to continue, is that we create evil out of our highest ideals and most noble aspirations. We so need to be heroic, to be on the side of God, to eliminate evil, to clean up the world, to be victorious over death, that we visit destruction and death on all who stand in the way of our heroic historical destiny. We scapegoat and create absolute enemies, not because we are intrinsically cruel, but because focusing our anger on an outside target, striking at strangers, brings our tribe or nation together and allows us to be a part of a close and loving in-group. We create surplus evil because we need to belong.

U.S. Parody of German Claim: God with Us
W.W.I

Holy War, Israeli Style
De La Torre. Columbia
© 1985 by Cartoonists and Writers Syndicate

It is within this context that the iconography of political propaganda must be understood. Whatever a society considers bad, wrong, taboo, profane, dirty, desecrated, inhumane, impure, will make up the epithets assigned to the enemy. The enemy will be accused of whatever is forbidden—from sadism to cannibalism. Study the face of the enemy and you will discover the political equivalent of Dante's circles of hell, the geography of evil, the shape of the shadow we deny.

The ritual and theological dimension of warfare is evident in primitive tribes in which the enemy is equated with the chaos that must be overcome yearly if the cosmos is to be sustained. As a blood rite, war follows naturally from the central assumptions of all primitive hunter-gatherer and agricultural peoples: death feeds life, blood must be shed, the seed must fall into the ground and die, to sustain life. To shed enemy blood was to recapitulate the cosmic drama, to participate in the sacrament by which life was renewed, to take part in the primal battle between the forces of creation and the forces of destruction. Quite often, as among the highland tribes of New Guinea, warfare ceased the moment any enemy blood had been spilled. One need not eliminate the enemy, only sacrifice the chaotic blood to complete the symbolic ritual of recreating the cosmos. This symbolism explains much of the spirit of game, conscious drama, and play, that accompanies primitive warfare. An Ojibway raiding party would sometimes ambush the Sioux and allow everybody except one man to escape, because a single death allowed the war ritual to be completed, the dances to be done, the purification to be completed, the victory to be celebrated. Other tribes, such as the Aztecs, who worshipped gods with insatiable appetites for human sacrifices, were forced to wage almost constant war on their enemies to secure the necessary victims.

The Western Judeo-Christian tradition of holy warfare goes back to the invasion of Canaan, when Yahweh supposedly commanded the Israelites to slay or enslave the native population and destroy its gods. The sin of the enemy was not only that it occupied the land that had been given to the chosen people, but that it worshipped "false" gods. Selective genocide—destroying all who refused to surrender—is justified in the Old Testament on religious grounds. The old divinities—Astarte, the Queen of Heaven, and Beëlzebub, the God of Fertility—were seen as idols and demons whose existence could not be tolerated by Yahweh, the jealous

Jihad
Sudhir Dar. The Hindustani Times
© 1985 by Cartoonists and Writers Syndicate

Crusade in Europe: In this sign conquer
U.S., W.W.II

God. Holy war was continued in the "new Canaan" by the New Israelites, the Puritans who believed themselves to have a "manifest destiny" to inhabit America the beautiful, from sea to shining sea, and who, therefore, considered the Native Americans "the bond slaves of Satan," "snares of the Devil," "the Devil's instruments."

In Islam, the *jihad* continued the tradition of holy war. It was the duty of all good Moslem princes to undertake a campaign yearly to extend the faith and to fight until all men bore witness that there was no God but Allah, and that his messenger was Mohammed. Warriors who died in sacred battle were immediately teleported into paradise. When the Crusades pitted Moslem against Christian, both agreed with the sacred paranoid assumption that the other was *the* enemy of the one, true, patriarchal, monotheistic God.

The imagery of holy war pictures our heroes as fighting "on the side of the angels," and the enemy as in league with the devil.

We like to think theocracies and holy wars ended with the coming of the Industrial Revolution and the emergence of secular culture in the West. But one look at twentieth-century propaganda dispels this notion. If anything, the ideology of holy war and the attribution of the symbols of absolute evil to the enemy has grown stronger in our supposedly secular century. That God has supposedly died has not prevented his use as a political sanction for warfare. In World War I, the Kaiser was pictured as the devil. In World War II, the Germans claimed "Gott mit uns," while in America we advertised, "In God we trust." Every nation with a Christian heritage has accused its enemies of being Christ killers, the crucifiers of the sacred. We pictured Hitler as a conspirator with the devil, and we went to war singing "Priase the Lord and Pass the Ammunition and we'll all stay free." Speaking about his experience of fighting in World War II, T. George Harris (founding editor of *American Health*) said,

> For me this was not a war of revenge. I was struggling to destroy an impersonal evil, not to inflict punishment. I stuck with God and prayed my way through scores of tight situations, repeating "not my will but Thine be done," over and over. If I repeated this prayer enough times I was able to relax and enjoy the battle. I was a vestal virgin warrior, an honest soldier dedicated to defeating God's enemy.

More recently we have witnessed the resurgence of militant Zionism and Islam. *Jihad* is alive and well in the Near East. Mu'ammar al-Khadafy of Libya carries on *jihad* by supporting terrorists and revolutionary movements because he considers Islamic peoples to be under attack ideologically and politically by the corrupt materialistic values of the West. And Palestine is once again sacred territory bequeathed by God to the Zionists, to be defended by the likes of General Sharon with all available means, not excluding massive bombings of civilians and massacres in Lebanon. Meanwhile, the Ayatollah Khomeini refers to the United States as "the Great Satan," and sends thousands of unarmed or poorly armed children across minefields into the waiting guns of Iraqi soldiers, all for the greater glory of God. Nowhere has the logic of holy war been more clearly stated than in a recent speech given by the Ayatollah Khomeini (on December 12, 1983 — anniversary of the Prophet Mohammed's birthday).

> If one permits an infidel to continue in his role as a corrupter of the earth, his moral suffering will be all the worse. If one kills the infidel, and thus stops him from perpetrating his misdeeds, his death will be a blessing to him. For if he remains alive, he will become more and more corrupt. This is a surgical operation commanded by God the all-powerful.
>
> War is a blessing for the world and for all nations. It is God who incites men to fight and to kill. The Koran says: "Fight until all corruption and all rebellion have ceased." The wars the Prophet led against the infidels were a blessing for all humanity. Imagine that we soon win the war [against Iraq]. That will not be enough, for corruption and resistance to Islam will still exist. The Koran says: "War, war until victory." A religion without war is an incomplete religion. If His Holiness Jesus — blessings upon him — had been given more time to live, he would have acted as Moses did, and wielded the sword. Those who believe that Jesus did not have "a head for such things," that he was not interested in war, see in him nothing more than a simple preacher, and not a prophet. A prophet is all-powerful. Through war he purifies the earth. The mullahs with corrupt hearts who say that all this is contrary to the teachings of the Koran are unworthy of Islam. Thanks to God, our young people are now, to the limits of their means, putting

The Atheistic Communists
Edmund Duffy. Baltimore Sun
Pulitzer Prize, 1930

God's commandments into action. They know that to kill the unbelievers is one of man's greatest missions.

And in sophisticated Washington, D.C., talk of apocalypse, Armageddon, and Empire of Evil, is once again heard in high places. President Reagan shares with the (self-named) Moral Majority a belief that we may be in the last days before God will bring the world to an end, and warns us against "the aggressive impulses of an evil empire." He identifies the Soviet Union as "the focus of evil in the modern world," and asks us "to pray for the salvation of all those who live in totalitarian darkness, pray they will discover the joys of knowing God." In emphasizing the dangers of godless communism, President Reagan continues a theme that has been central in our perceptions since before the Russian Revolution.

In the so-called secular world, our minds have learned to be embarrassed by overt religious claims made by any nation-state, and, thus, much of the visceral identification of our way of life with the divine truth has become covert and unconscious. Psychoanalysis has taught us that our deepest motives are often revealed in jokes, slips of the tongue, and exaggerations. Thus we should take political humor, in particular editorial cartoons, as revelations of the mythic assumptions a society makes about itself. The following story is an example.

Ronald Reagan, the president, became Ronald Reagan, the storyteller, Friday, to the delight of a highly partisan audience.

The president quoted a young marine lieutenant who had served in Grenada, as writing in the *Armed Forces Journal* that he noticed every news story about the "Grenada rescue mission" contained the line that Grenada produced more nutmeg than any place in the world.

"He decided that was a code," the President said. "He was going to break the code, and he did. He wrote back and said, "No. 1, Grenada produces more nutmeg than any place in the world.

"No. 2, the Soviets and the Cubans are trying to take Grenada.

"No. 3, you can't make good eggnog without nutmeg.

"No. 4, you can't have Christmas without eggnog.

"No. 5, the Soviets and the Cubans are trying to steal Christmas.

"No. 6, we stopped them."

As symbol and reality, Christmas unites the consciously affirmed and the unconscious theologies of American society—Christ and consumerism. Any threat to Christmas will be felt as an attack against what we hold most sacred: *Christian capitalism.* Nothing could function more effectively to identify the Communist as atheist than a "joke" justifying the Grenada invasion as a way of saving Christmas.

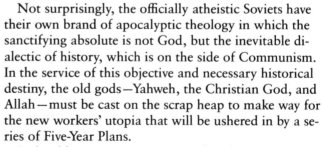

The Cosmonaut finds no God in the Heavens
U.S.S.R.

The Vicar of Wooton sanctifies British carnage
Germany, W.W.II

Not surprisingly, the officially atheistic Soviets have their own brand of apocalyptic theology in which the sanctifying absolute is not God, but the inevitable dialectic of history, which is on the side of Communism. In the service of this objective and necessary historical destiny, the old gods—Yahweh, the Christian God, and Allah—must be cast on the scrap heap to make way for the new workers' utopia that will be ushered in by a series of Five-Year Plans.

It should not escape our notice that the new apocalyptic mood and images are an inevitable consequence of our *advances* in weapons technology. Absolute weapons demand absolute enemies. Nothing less

1. U.S., 1942 **2.** "Only one man can save us from the monster of Bolshevism—Adolf Hitler." **3.** "What has the future in store for me?"—U.S.S.R., W.W.II **4.** U.S., W.W.II

1

3

2

4

5

1. U.S., W.W.II **2.** China, W.W.II **3.** U.S., W.W.II
4. "Down with the landlords who oppose the farmers."– China, post-W.W.II **5.** "Subscribe. (Buy Bonds.) They will surrender."– Italy, W.W.II

WHY SHOULD WE HELP COMMUNISTS KILL AMERICANS?

Mothers' Crusade For Victory Over Communism

We mothers, who are fighting to save our sons and our Republic, need your immediate financial and moral support. WILL YOU HELP US ??????? National Headquarters, Mothers' Crusade For Victory Over Communism, P. O. Box 943, Mesa, Arizona.

2   **3**   **4**

1. Mothers' crusade
2. "The Czar, the Priest and the Rich Man. They are the burden for the worker." Marxism focuses on the class enemy, the exploiting class

within every nation— U.S.S.R. **3.** "There is the guilt for the war." (the Jew)— Germany, W.W.II **4.** The Jew as metaenemy—France, W.W.II

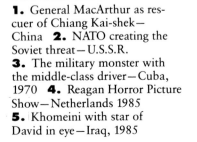

الغزو الايراني للعراق والغزو الصهيوني للبـــنان حلقة واحدة للتآمر على الامة العـــربية

مَصيرُ الغزاة الايرانيين القبرُ أوالاسر

1. General MacArthur as rescuer of Chiang Kai-shek—China 2. NATO creating the Soviet threat—U.S.S.R.
3. The military monster with the middle-class driver—Cuba, 1970 4. Reagan Horror Picture Show—Netherlands 1985
5. Khomeini with star of David in eye—Iraq, 1985

THE ENEMY AS ENEMY OF GOD

1

1. The Axis as Christ-killers—W.W.II **2.** "The atheists should be defeated."—Cambodia. Issued by the Lon Nol government, this implies that the government has the blessings of the Buddha and its enemies are outside aggressors—Vietnamese—and devils. In fact, at this time the enemies of the government were Khmer Rouge, who were mostly Cambodians.
3. U.S., W.W.II **4.** The Kaiser as Devil— U.S.S.R., W.W.I
5. "There will never be peace if the Red Devil is not dead. To tolerate Communism and to fight against Japan will destroy China."—Chinese Nationalists, 1941
6. Nazis as Christ- killers, crucifiers of the workers— pre-W.W.II

3

5

6

1. Onward Christian Soldiers.
When a soldier or revolutionary identifies with God or sav-
ior, killing the enemy becomes
a sacramental act—destroying
the enemy of God. **2.** Italian
and Nazi heroes kill the Russian hydra, the symbol of
chaos—Italy, W.W.II **3.** The
workers destroying the dragon
of capitalism—China
4. Onward Buddhist Soldiers—Cuba **5.** "The Czar is
for the bosses, and God for
those who lord it over the people." In Marxism the atheist
theme is turned on its head.
Religion is an illusion and opiate, and what is authentically
sacred is the dialectical movement of history toward the
socialist utopia.

THE ENEMY AS BARBARIAN

1.

2

3

4

1. Uncle Sam and President McKinley lead attack on the Chinese Boxers. The "heathen" Chinese, or the "yellow horde," have been recurring images whenever Westerners have faced Asian enemies — U.S., 1900   **2.** U.S., W.W.I
3. U.S., W.W.II   **4.** U.S., W.W.II

1. Pentagon (on hat). Human rights (glove). Against the background of these corpses you see the imprint of their "freedom." Their white gloves will not hide their black and bloody deeds—U.S.S.R.

2. This image was distributed by the Nazis in Holland during W.W.II to warn the Dutch against American troops, who are characterized as uncultured, blacks, gangsters, Jews, bankers, and bombers of cities. **3.** Note how the artist combines archetypal elements: the enemy is black, barbarian, and a rapist—Italy, 1942

4. "Only one danger threatens our culture and the integrity of our civilization—Bolshevism." Mussolini—Italy, W.W.II

UN SOLO PERICOLO MINACCIA LA NOSTRA CULTURA, LA NOSTRA INTE-GRITA' E LA NOSTRA CIVILTA'; E QUESTO PERICOLO E' IL BOLSCEVISMO

DALL'INTERVISTA CONCESSA ALL'INVIATO SPECIALE DEL "VOLKISCHER BEOBACHTER,, ROLAND STRUNK – 18 GENNAIO 1937-XV

Hitler and the Devil
Low. England. W.W.II

C.I.A. with Mafia Devil
U.S.S.R.

than the portrait of the enemy as absolute and total evil, incapable of change, can justify our possession and contemplated use of weapons that will totally annihilate the enemy and perhaps all other living things. We have by our ingenuity gained the power of the Devil—the power to destroy but not to create. But we cannot bear to face this image of ourselves, so we attribute it to our enemies.

One of the age-old functions of picturing the enemy as the enemy of God is to convert the guilt we naturally feel in killing into a source of pride, transform murder into devotion. As devil, demon, or myrmidon of evil, the enemy is possessed by an alien power. He fights not of his own will, but because he has been taken over by an alien spirit and is compelled by an illusion. Any warrior who kills such an enemy strikes a blow for truth and goodness and need have no remorse. Like the inquisitor who tortured heretics to make them confess their error, the warrior doing righteous battle against the enemies of God may come to see himself as a priest who actually saves his enemy from the grip of evil by killing him.

Holy wars and just causes invite warriors to view battle as sacred drama. The tradition is ancient. In the Hindu scripture (the Bhagavad-Gita), Arjuna, a member of the warrior caste, is reluctant to go into a battle in which he will be forced to fight against friends and relatives. The divine Krishna appears to him and calls

General Scott as Dragon Slayer
Civil War

Nazi as Dragon Slayer—"Wake up. Look out. Vote the Peoples Ticket"
Germany, pre-W.W.II

A theological argument, modern style
Kevin Kallaugher. England

him to do his duty without attachment. He assures him that from the perspective of the absolute, the contradictions and conflicts of history are meaningless, and that by participating in war with this knowledge he will be performing the yoga, the spiritual discipline, of the warrior and will reach enlightenment.

In a warfare state where *Homo hostilis* holds the reins of power, the warriors become the new priestly class. In modern times, the function of the shaman, the holy man who reads the signs, passes on the esoteric knowledge of the sacred, advises the tribe about the actions necessary to keep on the right side of God, has been usurped by the intelligence agency—by the CIA, KGB, and so on. There is a new mystical brotherhood of self-proclaimed experts who claim to have private knowledge of the "facts" on which we must base the decisions of war and peace. They read the "bird entrails"—computer printouts—that reveal what the enemy is doing. The military shamans who have the secret *gnosis* alone can decide whether we should unleash the nuclear arms that will destroy life. And, as is always the case, the layman is mystified and intimidated by the holders of this privileged information and is not allowed to question or assert an autonomous right to moral decision. Forget that our military shamans with their sacred technology for information gathering did not know that the Cuban people would support Castro and would fail to support the invaders at the Bay of Pigs, or that the Iranians would overthrow the Shah and return to a theocratic form of government, or even that Chairman Andropov was married.

THE ENEMY AS BARBARIAN

The Threat to Culture

Mexican Commander—G. Thomas 1846
Mexican-American War

Cult and culture are inevitably intertwined. Therefore the archetypal enemy will be perceived as atheist and barbarian, a denier of God and the destroyer of culture. He will be portrayed as rude, crude, and uncivilized. More than likely he will be an irrational, dirty member of a horde organized at best on the model of the ant heap. Usually the barbarian image is used by advanced cultures against simpler, less technologically complex peoples. To the Greeks, anyone who did not speak their language and share their customs was considered barbarian, and even Aristotle did not object to the slaughter of noncombatants and the selling of children of conquered peoples into slavery, because non-Hellenic people were by nature inferiors. For the Romans, everyone who lived beyond the pale of the civilizing law of the empire, especially the Germanic tribes, were barbarians. Fighting between unlike ethnic groups is most likely to invoke the image of the barbarian and to be more ferocious than between those who share some cultural similarity. A majority of American soldiers who had seen Japanese prisoners felt all the more like killing them; whereas more than half of those who had encountered German prisoners said, "It's too bad we have to be fighting them, they are men just like us."

As a rule of thumb, since the Industrial Revolution

Grant Hamilton 1898
Spanish-American War

The Turk as Barbarian—1897
U.S.

The German Giant as Barbarian
Belgium, W.W.I

The Bolshevik Giant
Germany, W.W.II

the technological nations have tended to view any peoples who did not have electricity, machine tools, and indoor plumbing as morally inferior and somehow lower on the scale of human evolution. Any peoples who still live as hunters and gatherers or by sustenance agriculture are in a state of nature, not yet dignified by the modern god Progress. Such "primitives" and "backward" people have always been exploited and patronized under the guise of "the white man's burden." Their reduced status is made clear by the less-than-human names they are assigned: *wog, nigger, gook, slant, heathen, pagan.*

If we think of the process of dehumanization on a scale of 1 to 100, the various barbarian images stand midway. The savage may be perceived as subhuman, but he or she still belongs to the human species, although as an inferior member who may rightfully be enslaved, used, or killed as necessary to advance the causes of progress and civilization. The archetype of the barbarian is made up of a cluster of related images. Propaganda posters often present a life-or-death choice between health and disease, civilization and savagery, light and darkness. The barbarous enemy is likely to be portrayed as either larger or smaller than normal. He may be shown as a bumbling giant who destroys cities by sheer size and stupidity, or as a little person whose slightness of stature suggests a moral midget, a stunted human. Sometimes he will be a cannibal or a wanton sadist.

The barbarian theme was widely used in World War II propaganda by all participants. Nazi anti-Semitic tracts contrasted the sunny, healthy Aryans to the inferior, dark races with contaminated blood—Jews, gypsies, Eastern Europeans. Blacks were portrayed as semigorillas, spoiling the Venus de Milo and other artistic achievements of European civilization. One poster used in Holland warned the inhabitants that their supposed "liberators" were a combination of KKK, jazz-crazed blacks, convicts, hangmen, and mad bombers. In turn, the United States frequently pictured the Germans as a Nazi horde of dark monsters on a mindless rampage.

Robert Ivie, who has made a study of the rhetoric and metaphors used to justify war, argues that images of savagery permeate the substance and style of the call to arms throughout American history. In the Revolutionary War, the British became monstrous savages,

The Barbarous Jap
U.S., W.W.II

"breaking out thirsting for American blood." In appealing to the U.S. people to go to war against Germany, FDR promised that the "rapid and united effort by all the people of the world who are determined to remain free will insure victory of the forces of justice and righteousness over the forces of savagery and barbarism." President Truman created a rhetoric for the cold war that "colored a picture of the enemy as brutal, bestial, domineering, inexorable, impersonal, blatant, blunt, immoral, powerful and destructive. Blunt, unrelenting brutality was the basic hue for international communism." Truman created this picture by a repetition of phrases such as "raw aggression," "communist slavery," "a dark and bloody path," "evil spirit," "iron rule of dictatorship," "puppet states," "the tide of atheistic communism," "use their people as cannon fodder," "the barbarian doctrine that might makes right," "an unlawful bandit attack on the South Korean Republic," "the challenge of the pagan wolves."

President Reagan has continued this rhetoric, focusing on the Soviet threat, of "totalitarian forces in the world who seek subversion and conflict around the globe to further their barbarous assault on the human spirit." According to Ivie, Reagan makes systematic use

The Russian Monster About to Escape—The crime against Europe
Germany, W.W.II

The Jew as terrorist and subversive
U.S.S.R., 1907.

Russian Caveman
Mitchell. The Australian
© 1985 by Cartoonists and Writers Syndicate

of eight categories of decivilizing rhetoric in the effort to paint the image of Soviet savagery:

1. The Soviets as natural menace who represent "darkness," "shadow," "tyranny," "grim, gray repression," "a gale of intimidation."
2. The Soviets as animals who are "untamed" and who "prey" on their neighbors.
3. The Soviets as primitives who "barbarously assault the human spirit," "use clubs against the Polish people."
4. The Soviets as machines, "instruments of destruction," "machines of war."
5. The Soviets as criminals who resort to "cruel extremes," and have erected a "murderous barrier" and are prepared "to commit any crime, to lie, to cheat."
6. The Soviets as mentally disturbed, a "world power of such deep fears, hostilities, and external ambitions."
7. The Soviets as fanatics and ideologues "immune to practical reason."
8. The Soviets as satanic and profane, "totalitarian evil."[7]

In a similar vein, Farrel Corcoran analyzes coverage of the Soviet Union by the three major American news magazines, *Time, Newsweek,* and *U.S. News & World Report,* and finds that the words most often used to characterize the Russians are "*savages, dupes, adventurers, despots,* and *barbarians,* and their methods of behavior as *brutal, treacherous, conniving, unmanly,*

The Fifth Horseman
Oliphant, by Pat Oliphant. Copyright, 1984,
Universal Press Sindicate. Used by permission.
All rights reserved.

46

New style barbarians
Berry. The Star. Johannesburg, South Africa. © 1985 by Cartoonists and Writers Syndicate.

aggressive and *animalistic*" (italics added).[8] These impressions are created by descriptions of the "shuffling" feet of Moscow crowds waiting in the cold, damp winter to get into Lenin's tomb, "raw and freezing winds," "brutality of the climate," "stolidity" of the people, the "vast and unknowable" character of the land, the "politically anesthetized" population, the "Byzantine power politics," the peasant origins of the leaders, "the gray and tired old men who run the Kremlin," the "boorish" character of the people.

From the American media I would never have guessed that the sun often shines on Red Square, that there are apple orchards, golden-domed churches, and modernistic buildings within the ancient walls of the Kremlin. And, at times, laughter and a modicum of goodwill.

Among army personnel, the barbarian image remains. The Soviet Union is considered a backward country with a totally repressive government whose only form of technological achievement is in weapons, whose advanced designs have been mostly stolen from the United States. One army captain recently told me, "We think of the Soviet soldier as some poor peasant who is in the army not by choice, but because he is forced to. He wouldn't fight unless his leaders made him. But he is like a rattlesnake; he is dangerous if you step on him." Sophisticated army films picturing "The Threat" (the only category under which the Soviets are dealt with by the military), show a more complex picture of the Russian military. But the stereotype remains.

Among other disadvantages, such degraded images of the enemy lead us to underestimate their intelligence and commitment, and they give us sanction to use brutal tactics that reduce us to the level of barbarism.

THE GREEDY ENEMY

The Appetite for Empire

The enemy is insatiable, has no sense of proper limits or legitimate boundaries. He opens his gullet, swallows his neighbors, and becomes bloated with the spoils of conquest. Give him an inch, and he will take a mile. So best stand up to his aggression now. Remember Munich! In propaganda, the insatiable enemy is often represented by images taken from our earliest associations of oral aggression. He bites, chews, and swallows his victims. His eating habits are not the civilized tasting of the gourmet, but the gluttonous gorging of an animal. He is the toothy monster of fairytales and nightmares.

We, by contrast, are restrained. Like good adults, we are satisfied with what is legitimately ours. We respect our neighbors' boundaries and and do not meddle in the internal affairs of other sovereign nations. Upon occasion, of course, we find it necessary to come to the aid of beleaguered governments who request our aid. Or to spread the mantle of progress and bring the blessings of civilization and justice to backward nations.

According to the Marxist gospel, private property is theft and money the root of all evil. Greed is the result of the exploitation of one class by another. The enemy is not a single nation but the capitalist elite of every nation. Soviet propaganda almost always caricatures Uncle Sam, the archcapitalist, as a bloated banker with dollar signs for eyes. He milks the resources from underdeveloped countries and tramples on the weak. And the elite of the elite—the military-industrial complex—steals the food from the American lower classes. Money that should go to social programs is gobbled up by the Pentagon. An argument one frequently hears in the Soviet Union to buttress their claim that Communism is exempt from the motive of greed is "We do not have a military-industrial complex where an elite makes a

FDR: The World Robber
Germany, W.W. II

1917 German Military Power
Jay Darling. Des Moines Register

Communist Snake Swallowing Asia
James Dobbins. Boston Herald-American
1975

Who is Greedy?
Don Wright. Miami News, 1976

profit from the arms race, because we do not have private ownership. Therefore, we obviously manufacture weapons only because we are forced to defend ourselves. If we support wars of national liberation, it is only to hasten the day when there will be international justice and an end to greed. And in the eventual workers' utopia, unnatural desires will vanish and each will contribute according to his abilities and receive according to his needs."

According to capitalist propaganda, communism is only a new ideology for the exploitation of the masses by a new ruling class. The Soviet commissars are no less greedy than the Czars. The appetite for empire is obvious from their expansionistic policies. Wherever there is trouble in the world, they meddle. The U.S.S.R. itself is a loose union of slave satellite states and ethnic minorities held together against their will by a repressive central government. And the Russian elite, far from practicing equality, grab the caviar, enjoy plushy

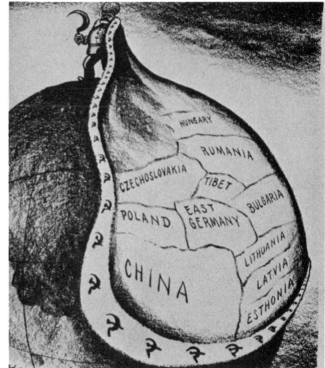

Fitzpatrick. St. Louis Post-Dispatch

49

dachas, purchase Western goods in special hard-currency stores, and leave the workers a diet of stale bread, faulty televisions, and cheap vodka (which replaces religion as the opiate of the masses).

THE ENEMY AS CRIMINAL

Anarchists, Terrorists, and Outlaws

WANTED!

by Tokyo

ANY MILITARY INFORMATION YOU MAY HAVE!

Enemy as Outlaw
U.S., W.W.II

When modern nations go to war, their propaganda usually distinguishes between the governments and leaders of the nations they oppose and the people of those nations. Thus recent U.S. propaganda has sought to drive a wedge between the Sandinista government and the Nicaraguan people, and the CIA has instructed propagandists to play on this theme:

> The basic objective of a preconditioning campaign is to create a negative "image" of the common enemy; e.g., describe the managers of collective government entities as trying to treat the staff the way "slave" foremen do. The police mistreat the people like the communist "Gestapo" does. The government officials of National Reconstruction are puppets of Russian-Cuban imperialism. . . . Create a favorable opinion of our movement. Through local and national history, make it clear that the Sandinista regime is "foreignizing," "repressive," and "imperialistic," and that even though there are some Nicaraguans within the government, point out that they are "puppets" of the power of the Soviets and Cubans, i.e., of foreign power.[9]

The common people are innocent victims who do not want war, but their government is corrupt, illegitimate, and violent.

In 1984 when I visited both Nicaragua and the Soviet Union, I heard the familiar litany repeated a thousand times: "We love the American people but we hate the American government." One way we deny our common responsibility for war is by the self-justifying illusion that people are peaceful and only leaders are violent. This dogma yields three corollary axioms:

1. We harbor no hatred against their people.
2. In going to war, governments do not express the will of the people.
3. We (the people) are good. They (the leaders) are evil.

Modoc Indians as Outlaws in Chains
U.S. Army Photograph

From these assumptions the image of the enemy as criminal or outlaw is constructed. The antiphonal litany of propaganda differs little from war to war:

We are law abiding.	They are criminals, outlaws.
We respect our agreements and treaties, and abide by the rule of international law.	They are liars, cheaters, thieves, and opportunists who break treaties whenever it is to their advantage.
We are peace keepers. Our use of force is a police action designed to protect law and order.	They are violent, gangsters, a criminal band. They follow a policy of adventurism.
We stand for justice and civil rights.	They brutalize, repress, and tyrannize both their neighbors and their own people.
Our leaders govern with the consent of the people.	Their leaders are usurpers with no popular support who will eventually be overthrown.
We give foreign aid.	They export revolution.

In the absence of effective world government and international law, each nation will always seek to justify its own use of violence and condemn its neighbor's. When the Soviets "brutally crush" a popular uprising in Hungary, the United States and all "free nations" call on the World Court in the Hague to condemn their actions. When the U.S.-supported Contras mine Nicaraguan ports and terrorize the population, the United States refuses in advance to abide by any judgment of the same court. The doctrine of national sovereignty is, in effect, a nationalistic claim to exercise a right to a monopoly on the use of violence, to legitimize one's own use of "power" and to delegitimize one's enemy's use of "criminal violence." The CIA conducts covert actions that sometimes involve "terminating" an enemy, while the KGB's "activities run the gamut from murder, espionage, and terrorism."[10] We may hire operatives with Mafia connections to eliminate Castro, but we do not, like Colonel Khadafy, use "hit squads."

In the present political climate the label "terrorist" is in high favor among propaganda makers. Established governments, such as that of South Africa, habitually

Pancho Villa as Criminal
Donahey. Cleveland Plain Dealer

Cesare. U.S., W.W.I, 1916

**Churchill as Gangster
Anti-propaganda**
England, W.W.II

designate any use of arms by a disenfranchized minority
"terrorism." The Soviet Union regularly accuses the
United States in such statements as: "The Reagan administration has chosen terrorism as a method of conducting affairs with other states and peoples."[11] The
United States returns the charge. President Reagan suggests that the Soviet Union supports a terrorist network
of five "outlaw states"—Iran, Libya, North Korea, Cuba
and Nicaragua—that are "run by the strangest collection of misfits, 'Looney Tunes' and squalid criminals
since the advent of the Third Reich."[12] The Sandinistas
are singled out as the sponsors of terror in El Salvador
and as the principle refuge for international terrorists.
Their enemies, the United States-sponsored Contras
who are responsible for killing thousands of Nicara-
guans are, by contrast, designated "freedom fighters."
Israel regularly accuses the Palestine Liberation Organization of terrorist tactics but justifies its own bombings
of civilians as legitimate retaliation. The United States

The New Outlaws
Plantu. LeMonde, France
© 1985 by Cartoonists and Writers Syndicate

media almost universally condemned the Shi'ite terrorists who hijacked TWA flight 847 and murdered a hostage but ignored the revelation that the CIA had trained the terrorists in Lebanon who placed a car bomb that killed eighty people and wounded two hundred, or that Israel had seized 1200 Shi'ite hostages and moved them to Israel where they were held incommunicado, denied even a Red Cross visit.[13]

Charges and countercharges about disrespect for civil rights are a regular part of Soviet American relations. The Western press campaigns in support of dissident physicist Andre Sakharov and his wife. The Soviet press has championed the cause of Native American leader Leonard Peltier, who was charged with murdering two FBI agents in a shootout on a Sioux reservation in South Dakota—a conviction some civil rights groups in this country, along with *Pravda,* say is a prosecution

Rogue's Gallery
Behrendt. Netherlands
© 1985 by Cartoonists and Writers Syndicate

for political reasons. The charge that the U.S.S.R. represses its non-Russian ethnics is countered by cartoons showing the FBI as the ally of the Ku Klux Klan in repressing American blacks. Americans claim Soviets violate human rights. Soviets regularly emphasize the crime and lawlessness of U.S. society, the "cult of violence and cruelty," which is inculcated in Americans by a "wolfish law in which the strong devour the weak" and by the popular glorification of legendary criminals such as Bonnie and Clyde, and Al Capone.

THE ENEMY AS TORTURER

Sadism in Mass

torture

This is the method of the enemy

WE FIGHT TO BUILD A FREE WORLD

Torture: the method of the Enemy
U.S., W.W. II

The torturous and atrocious character of the enemy follows as a natural consequence of his barbarism. We cannot expect subhuman creatures to have refined sensibilities or to play by the rules of civilized warfare. However, since these images play such a large part in motivating civilian populations to support war, they deserve special attention in the iconography of the hostile imagination.

Babies on bayonets, the slaughter of civilians, and the systematic torture of prisoners form a regular part of the rhetoric justifying warfare. The enemy is a sadist who delights in inflicting pain on others. Before going into the Sudetenland, the Germans circulated stories of atrocities committed against German people dwelling there. Accounts of German soldiers cutting off the arms of women and children in France and Belgium were widely reported by the British press in World War I. When an international commission investigated and found no evidence that the supposed incidents had happened, the retractions were given scant attention. Atrocity stories are necessary to fan the flames of war. Armenian nationalists still keep alive the memory of the slaughter of Armenians by Turks a half-century ago.

Following the invasion of Grenada, the Soviet press charged, "There are many accounts of the bloody deeds of American soldiers also on the Island of Grenada, where they arranged a real slaughterhouse among the civilian population. Killing, robbing and committing outrages, they confirm their way of life." A recent Soviet hate-America propaganda campaign has emphasized that "in the modern world, love for the socialist Father-

Englishman: "You did this"
Poland, W.W.II

land is impossible without class hatred. Hatred for the enemy is the guardian of patriotic love." The January 1984 issue of *Military Knowledge* carried a picture of American soldiers sounding off with an explanation that they were comparable to legendary Russian monsters. Says the article,

> One can boldly and without exaggeration call these cutthroats in the U.S. uniform monsters. And what, in fact, is human in these frenzied, teethbaring physiognomies, in these eyes, the eyes of killers and rapists? What can be sacred for such fellows? Such people, without having a doubt and giving a thought, will go to any cruelty, any crime. They will not be moved by pity on seeing the tears of a child, the desperate cry of a dying woman, their hands will not falter in killing a defenseless old man.[14]

The Bolshevik barbarian
Italy, W.W.II

Meanwhile, the American public remembers the monumental cruelty of the Stalin purges, continues to suspect that the Soviet Union is just one big Gulag concentration camp, and regularly reports Soviet atrocities in Afghanistan. Fred Schwartz, a leaders of the Christians' Anti-Communist Crusade, gives the right-wing view of the Communist as sadist:

> We can trust the Communists to manifest pure, Marxist-Leninist "love." One of the best pictures of Marxist-Leninist "love" was revealed in the boast made by Klementi Voroshilov, now President of

DeGaulle as Hitler the Archsadist
U.S.S.R.

Russia, to William Bullitt, America's first ambassador to the Soviet Union. At a banquet in Russia in 1934, Voroshilov told Bullitt that in 1919 he persuaded eleven thousand Czarist officers at Kiev to surrender by promising them that, if they surrendered, they, their wives, and their families, would be permitted to return to their homes. When they surrendered, he executed the eleven thousand officers and all their male children, and sent the wives and daughters into the brothels for the use of the Russian army. He mentioned in passing that the treatment they received in the brothels was such that none of them lived for more than three months. . . . Voroshilov was merely acting in obedience to the dictates of Marxist-Leninist "love," believing as he believed, he acted in a truthful, righteous, and loving manner. There he stood, one of history's anointed, entrusted with the destiny of world con-

Stalin as Hitler
Fitzpatrick. St. Louis Post-Dispatch

Israel as Nazi
U.S.S.R.

Contemporary Greek poster keeping alive the memory of the Armenian massacre by Turks a half century ago.

quest and human regeneration. There stood a group of male and female animals. . . . His duty lay clearly before him. As a Communist he had no choice. He was nothing; these people were nothing; the will of history was everything. To the executioners went all the males, and to the brothels went all the females. The Red Army was strengthened, world conquest came a day nearer, human regeneration a little closer, and Voroshilov had a conscience as clear as spring water, and a sense of duty nobly done.[15]

It should go without saying that the charges of torture and atrocities made by one nation against another are almost always true in substance if not in detail. Amnesty International has documented enough of the horrendous history of modern sadism to show us that in times of war and/or political crisis, most nations resort to wanton cruelty. No nation-state is innocent of torture and atrocity.

The propaganda tactic that identifies the enemy as torturer is based on a series of unstated assumptions that are designed to give sanction to our use of violence and to delegitimize others:

1. The enemy commits torture, atrocity, and murder because he is a sadist who enjoys killing.
2. We use surgical or strategic violence only because we are forced to by the enemy.
3. Killing is justified so long as one does not take pleasure in it and it is done in a clean manner—preferably from the antiseptic distance of the bomber or an artillery position where one does not see and cannot make moral discriminations between combatants and noncombatants. For instance, the saturation bombing of hamlets in the free-fire zone in Vietnam was legitimate, but the face-to-face slaughter of the population of MyLai was a "war crime."

A particularly transparent illustration of the principle of the dual standard was Britain's treatment of prisoners in Northern Ireland. A committee appointed to investigate charges of torture concluded that the abuses to which prisoners were subjected in an effort to extract information only constituted "physical ill treatment" but not brutality, because "we consider that brutality is an inhuman or savage form of cruelty, and that cruelty implies a disposition to inflict suffering, coupled with indifference to, or pleasure in, the victim's pain."[16]

THE ENEMY AS RAPIST

Woman as Bait and Trophy

The Jew as Seducer
Germany, W.W.II

Closely associated with the charge of barbarism is the portrayal of the enemy as rapist and destroyer of motherhood.

As rapist, the enemy is unadulterated lust defiling unambiguous innocence. Our women are too pure to find an enemy sexually desirable or lovable, and must be protected from the enemy's uncivil passions. As Susan Griffin says,

> Women who are not protected by men are viewed as sexual objects; in this role they are simply part of the "booty" of war, to be raped, owned and used. Typically, in male cross-group dialogue, "my" women are good and protected; "your" women are bad and deserve to be raped. In fact, then, there are two male-controlled roles traditionally assigned women: Good Mothers who are protected and Bad Whores who are punished.[17]

In Nazi propaganda the defiled Jew lurked in the shadows waiting to seduce or rape Aryan girls. In the mythology of the Ku Klux Klan, the black man has an insatiable lust for white women. In American war posters, the rapist is the Jap and the Nazi.

As the destroyer of motherhood, the enemy threatens the sacred Madonna-and-Child. Here it is not the woman as sexual object who is threatened, but as nurturer, the guardian of home, hearth, and family.

In the iconography of warfare, women play only a minor part. Writing about warfare is one of the few places where the male bias of our language is appropriate. War is largely a man's game. Because it is necessary for us to erase from the face of the enemy any characteristic that might trigger our identification or compassion, the enemy is seldom pictured as female. At the very least, enemy women remain desirable as sexual objects. Occasionally in circumstances of guerrilla warfare where women and children take an active part in the manufacture of arms and in actual combat, they will be included in the image of the enemy. But even where women and children are in fact killed as a matter of policy, as in the fire bombings of Dresden, they are not included in the official propaganda images. It is almost universally considered less than heroic to make war against women and children, even though it is almost universally practiced.

In actual unspoken fact, woman plays another un-

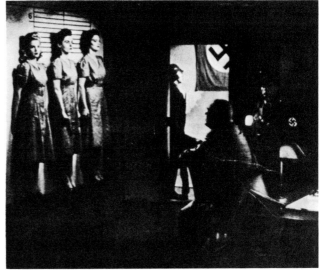

NO MERCY

acknowledged role in warfare: she is prize and bait. To the victor belong the spoils, the chief of which is the enemy's women. The appeal to sexual adventure is a *sine qua non* in motivating men to go to war. In its mildest form, this is the promise of cohabiting with strange women. In its stronger form, it is the covert permission given to "normal" men only in enemy lands to satisfy their rapacious appetite and to vent their hostility on women without consequences. The opportunity to seduce or rape has been, and remains, one of the perennial appeals of war:

> You take a group of men and put them in a place where there are no round-eyed women. They are in an all-male environment. Let's face it. Nature is nature. There are women available. Those women are of another culture, another color, another society. You don't want a prostitute. You've got an M-16. What do you need to pay for a lady for? You go down to the village and take what you want. I saw guys who I believe never had any kind of sex with a woman before in that kind of scene. They'd come back a double veteran. [Definition: Having sex with a woman and then killing her.] Being in that kind of environment, you give a guy a gun and strange things happen.[18]

Communist as "Free Love" Advocate
Thomas Nast. U.S., 1878

Women play other important roles in the symbolism used to sanctify war. Traditionally, she is the muse who stands behind the warrior and the nurse who tends him when he is wounded. She encourages, inspires men in war. She is the spectator who applauds bravery, the invisible spirit audience before whom heroic acts are performed. And the mother who waits and prays for her son's return. As such she is usually a spectral creature, wispy, pure, and ethereal. Occasionally, she seems to promise sexual favors to the warrior: "She wants you—to serve your country." In the strange dialectic we have created by the gender divisions necessary to condition men to kill and women to nurture, women seldom are the advocates of war, yet they remain excited by the perfume of violence. Until recently the soldier in uniform, the manly warrior has been a sex object. Machismo and the martial model of masculinity have proven sufficiently attractive to women to motivate many men to join the regiment. Part of the sense of betrayal experienced by Vietnam veterans came from the feminine rage they encountered. Instead of being greeted as heroes they were "baby killers" and tainted warriors.

THE ENEMY AS BEAST, REPTILE, INSECT, GERM

Sanctions for Extermination

In the scale of dehumanization, we drop from the midpoint of the subhuman barbarian to the nonhuman,

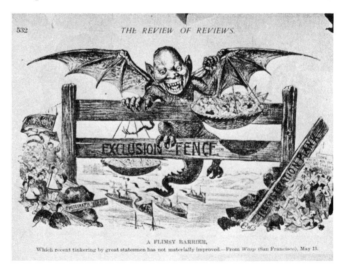

Chinese as Bat-Dragon
U.S., 1893

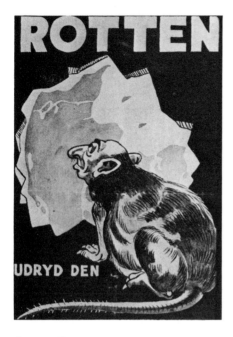

Jew as Rat
Germany, W.W. II

German as Tuberculosis
France, W.W. I

from the savage to the animal. "A running dog of capitalism," "a Nazi swine," a "Jap rat," a "Commie bear," are clearly dangerous, irrational animals, capable of cunning, whom we are morally justified in killing without mercy. The lower down in the animal phyla the images descend, the greater sanction is given to the soldier to become a mere exterminator of pests. The anti-Semitic propaganda that reduced the Jew to louse or rat was an integral part of the creation of the extermination camps. When Franz Stangl, the commandant of Treblinka, was asked why the killing of the Jews was organized in such a way as to achieve the maximum humiliation and dehumanization of the victims, he replied, "To condition those who actually had to carry out the policies. To make it possible for them to do what they did."[19] The Jew was reduced to "cargo" by being shipped in cattle cars, to contaminated pest that should be exterminated by poison gasses originally designed as pesticides.

The use of bestial images seems initially to be one of the better ways of dehumanizing an enemy because it allows soldiers to kill without incurring guilt. But the problem is that it allows the warrior-become-exterminator little sense of dignity or pride in his skill in battle. There is little emotional purgation gained from the slaughter of such an enemy—no heroic sparring with a worthy opponent, no cosmic drama of a

Arafat as Rat
Scrawls. Atlanta Constitution. Used by special permission

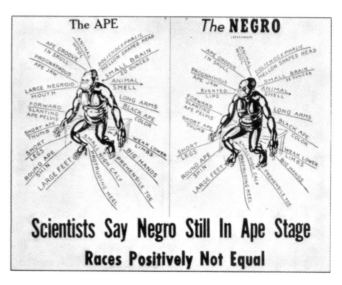

Black as Ape
American Eugenics Party, U.S., 1970

Scot as Gorilla
Germany, W.W.I

battle against enemies of God, no wrestling with barbarian giants. Only an escalating brutality and insensitivity to suffering and death.

Glenn Gray recounts an incident from World War II:

> When a Japanese soldier was "flushed" from his hiding place well behind the lines of combat, "the unit, made up of relatively green troops, was resting and joking. But they seized their rifles and began using him as a live target while he dashed frantically around the clearing in search of safety. The soldiers found his movements uproariously funny and were prevented by their laughter from making an early end of the unfortunate man. Finally, however, they succeeded in killing him, and the incident cheered the whole platoon, giving them something to talk and joke about for days afterward. In relating this story . . . the veteran emphasized the similarity of the enemy soldier to an animal. None of the American soldiers apparently ever considered that he may have had human feelings of fear and the wish to be spared.[20]

Such incidents were common in Vietnam:

> We had this one dude who would go out shooting people, then yell "Snake." Like, don't worry, I just killed a snake next to the trail. We come across this

Nazi snake
U.S.S.R., W.W.II

China as Shark
Coco. Taiwan
© 1985 by Cartoonists and Writers Syndicate

old papa-san dying in the dirt in a hooch. Mama-san is there leaning over him. The dude walks up, pulls out that .45, and blows the fucker's brains out. Says to me, "I was just helping the fucker out." Then he turns around and shoots this mother and her baby. Steps outside the hooch and says, "Snake."[21]

At the extreme end of the spectrum of natural pests, the enemy becomes a germ. In World War I, when tuberculosis was still a common disease, the injunction to fight TB and fight the Hun were often combined in a single poster. More recently, now that cancer has risen to the surface of our consciousness as the symbol of the evil *par excellence,* we are told that communism is a "creeping cancer."

Tito
U.S.S.R.

Indira Ghandi
Farhat. Egypt
© 1985 by Cartoonists and Writers Syndicate

Ortega (Nicaragua) as Wasp
Behrendt. Het Parool, Netherlands
© 1985 by Cartoonists and Writers Syndicate

In passing, we should note that the way modern allopathic medicine thinks about disease and the way propagandists think about warfare bear a systematic similarity. Disease is largely considered something that strikes us from the outside. The germ, like the enemy, is an outside aggressor that will overwhelm us if we allow our defenses to wane. Cancer, like communism, is an irrational force against which we launch crusades and wars. Evil comes from without.

THE ENEMY AS DEATH

The Ultimate Threat

War is always portrayed as a cosmic drama, a battle between Life and Death, Light and Darkness. Propaganda relegates the enemy to the role of agent of death. He is the ancient Grim Reaper, cutting down youth in its prime, running rampant over the land, mowing the population down. Or he is one of the Four Horsemen of the Apocalypse, in recent time shown seated astride an airborne steed—a Nazi or British bomber. His face is reduced to a skull, his body a dangling skeleton. We,

The Indomitable Spirit
Low. England, W.W.II

Franco,du fliegst höher als Blanco

Franco as Death Dealer
Germany, 1930s

Death on a Black Horse
Jose Guadalupe Posada.
Mexico, 1910

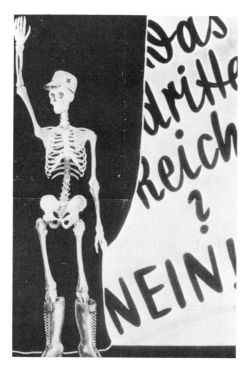

"The Third Reich? No!"
Anti-Nazi Germany, 1930s

the bearers of "the indomitable spirit," are the angels of life.

Since war deals in death, and death seems to be to the rational mind an inevitable consequence of mortality, a part of every human's destiny, the portrayal of the enemy as a death bringer seems too obvious to bear mentioning. At its simplest, propaganda must switch the blame for the massive suffering and death from us to them. Although we also deal in death, we are not to blame because we are forced to defend ourselves against an enemy who is the incarnation of death. But there is a much more profound, unconscious significance to the

死鲁门和他的上帝

·范滋德·

death imagery, that we can probe in greater detail only in dealing with the psychology of enmity. A Martian observer of the human scene would undoubtedly report that Earthlings each generation engage in death festivals, ritual potlatch sacrifices, in which the most vital young people of at least two nations are sacrificed in battles in a compulsive effort to defeat death. Each side in the conflict portrays the other as death incarnate, and seems to operate under the spell of an illusion that if it could kill its momentary enemy it could somehow magically destroy death. For the moment we will only note this cruel paradox of human behavior—our propensity to fight for peace, hate for love, kill for life.

U.S. with skeletal Hitler
China

THE ENEMY AS WORTHY OPPONENT

Heroic Warfare

War is as necessary as the struggle of the elements in nature. . . . It gives a biologically just decision since its decisions rest on the very nature of things.
Gen. van Bernhardi, 1912

Since the beginning of recorded warfare, there has been one tradition that seeks to dignify rather than dehumanize the enemy. In the heroic or chivalric tradition, war has been considered the most noble of all human activities and the warrior the most elevated human type.

The ideal of heroic warfare is rooted in a metaphysic of struggle. Reality itself is an *agon*—a contest or game—an ontological wrestling match between light and dark, good and evil, yin and yang. In Greek mythology, the gods themselves are pictured at war with each other. So if, in the divine scheme of things, Zeus must fight with Poseidon and the very elements of air, fire, earth, and water, are in constant struggle to maintain their equilibrium, then human beings must also be willing to enter into battle. Under the impact of social Darwinism, thinkers such as Oswald Spengler and Nietzsche considered man a natural "beast of prey" whose martial instincts ensured the survival of the fittest, or at least, the fiercest. Life feeds on life. Therefore the warrior is a human embodiment of a cosmic principle, and warfare is a kind of sacrament in which men reenact the struggle between the forces of order and the forces of chaos. Combat is a ritual of purification, a means by which we progress or evolve to a higher form of life.

"Dying Gaul"
Note the dignity the artist gives to the dying enemy soldier.
Epigonos 220 B.C.
Capitolini Museum, Rome
Photo: Max Hirmer

Our spiritualization of hostility . . . consists in a profound appreciation of having enemies. . . . A new creation — the new Reich, for example, needs enemies more than friends: in opposition alone does it feel itself necessary. Our attitude to the "internal enemy" is no different; here too we have spiritualized hostility. . . . The price of fruitfulness is to be rich in internal opposition; one remains young only so long as the soul does not stretch itself and desire peace.
Friedrich Nietzsche,
Twilight of the Idols

The notion of heroic warfare goes back at least as far as the Trojan Wars, and the reports in the Iliad of the epic battles of Achilles and Agamemnon. In Japan, the samurai developed a code of honorable combat and a variety of martial arts such as ju jitsu, which required respect for the opponent. In the West, we saw the flowering of the heroic ideal in the age of chivalry when the likes of King Arthur and the Knights of the Round Table jousted for glory and the admiration of high-born ladies. In modern times the professional military in the Prussian army, the English regiment, the RAF, and so on, have continued to view combat as a kind of deadly game between worthy opponents.

When war is viewed as a game, divine or secular, a good enemy is as necessary as a friend. There is no glory to be won in exterminating a rat or slaughtering an inferior species of subhuman beings. Thus, within the heroic tradition, warrior and enemy form a relationship of mutual respect, compassion, and even admiration. Since the motive of the heroic warrior is to win fame, glory, and demonstrate his courage, he desires a good enemy. By its very nature heroic combat is aristocratic, individualistic, and rule governed. Honorable warriors face each other on a footing of equality, having agreed on the rules: the choice of weapons, the conditions of truce, starting and ending of warfare, the treatment of captured combatants, and so on. These conditions may be stringent beyond anything modern pragmatists can understand. There was, for instance, a convention that siege could not begin without a formal ceremony. The French once lodged a formal complaint that the English siege band included violins and such

Knights in Single Combat
13th Century

instruments were not permitted. (The only corollary in modern warfare is the prohibition by the Geneva Convention of bagpipes.)

To our modern eyes, heroic warfare seems more a game than serious. It is hard for us to understand why so much of the history of warfare should involve set battles where armies agreed to meet on specific fields and fight with a limited repertoire of weapons. Or to believe that World War I was won on the playing fields of Eton, where the British turned out officers who led their men into combat with a baton and refused to carry weapons because killing was not gentlemanly. Nor in an age when technological "progress" alone has determined what weapons we will use can we understand the decision of certain samurai to ban gunpowder and guns from honorable combat because they allowed the vulgar and undisciplined to be more effective in killing than the most heroic swordsman. It helps to remember that premodern wars were not as massive or bloody as ours. Not all people showed the good sense of the New Guinea tribes who called off any battle when rain threatened to ruin their elaborate feather headdresses. But wars between Greek city-states, as Arthur Darby Nock at Harvard was fond of saying, "were only slightly more dangerous than American football."

The "game" of war, for a while formalized by the Greeks in the regular *agon* of the Olympic games, has always been highly prized by certain men. It has received praise no less effusive than sex or love as the highest of human experiences. And for similar reasons. In the heat of battle, men forget themselves, surrender to their pas-

Kuniyoshi's prints helped to popularize and romanticize the samurai warrior.

Analytical battle picture showing organization of armies
Battle of Lutzen, 1632

sions, transcend their small egos, and often sacrifice themselves for those they love. Most who have participated in battle speak of the "joy" of battle in which men lose their calculating egos and move with a grace they have not known before. "The most intense experience of my life." "The time I was most alive." These are common tributes paid to war.

Heroic warfare gives us our most humanized face of the enemy. In the first place, the heroic warrior must know his enemy. A swordsman or knight who went out to battle with a stereotype would be poorly prepared to fight. Professional warriors make an intricate study of the tactics and styles of those they intend to join in combat. They try to get inside their minds, learn how they think. Empathy and imagination are required. Even in modern warfare professionals spend much of their time in military academies studying the enemy's mind. Field Manual No. 100-5, *Operations,* explains in detail how the U.S. Army must conduct campaigns and

Aikido, a Martial Art
Jean Maggrett

*Play makes
gentle men
love limits.
In the game
love rules.*

Every advance in military technology has marked a retreat from honor.
Sandor McNab

battles in order to win. It describes operational doctrine and is no doubt studied by Soviet strategists as carefully as we study the Soviet Military Encylopedia. American aviators studied the tactics of the Red Baron as carefully as the Miami Dolphins will study the game plan of the Forty-niners. War may not be the most intimate human relationship, as one World War II film says it is, but nothing except love moves us to take others so seriously, to explore their mind, their motives, give them such intricate attention. Warriors and lovers have much in common. In fact, war might be seen as a kind of homosexual ritual, a kind of perverse love affair for men who cannot love unless they can hit.

From empathy comes a measure of compassion. To know in detail is to limit hate, perhaps even to abolish it. Training in hatred may be a necessary part of inducing civilian populations to make the sacrifices necessary for war, and of the military process of turning civilians into soldiers, but it plays a much less central role in either the heroic or the professional soldier. The professional soldier, who views himself in the heroic and chivalric tradition, considers his enemy a fellow professional, a comrade in arms to be outwitted and conquered but not humiliated. In World War II, Field Marshall Rommel insisted on the proper treatment of prisoners, on honoring the Geneva Convention. So long as the enemy is fighting, he may be destroyed mercilessly. But once he is conquered, he must be treated humanely. The professional soldier may understand his opponent's motives more instinctively than those of his own political superiors or civilians.

Look closely at what is required to conduct successful warfare and you will find a contradiction built into the way we think about the enemy. To fight and kill we require both information and misinformation, both respect and disdain, both truth and falsehood, both honor and dishonor, both an empathic and a degraded portrait of the enemy. To be effective strategists we must know the mind and personality of the enemy no less than his tactical capabilities. To be effective killers we must dehumanize the enemy so that we will not be burdened by guilt nor crippled by compassion. In large measure Hitler was defeated on the Eastern front because he lacked appreciation of the Russian psyche. His inflated image of the Aryans and deflated image of Slavs blinded him to the knowledge that Mother Russia always embraced her enemies, waited, endured, suffered, and finally froze and defeated them in her vast, wintry

German Duelists—Honorable Enemies

bosom. Likewise his loathing of the Jew cost him the genius of Einstein and possibly the atomic weapons that might have allowed him to win the war. In short, he broke the first rule of war: know your enemy.

The essence of the heroic tradition is honorable obedience to rules limiting the scope and methods of warfare. In one age this may involve prearranged battles on mutually agreed-on fields where armies face each other like tin soldiers lined up by obsessively neat generals. In another age it may mean only the agreement to prohibit the use of poison gas and chemical agents or to respect truces. Until recently the professional code confined warfare to combatants. Honorable warriors did not kill women, children, and other civilians. Of course, atrocities have always accompanied warfare, but they have been considered beneath the dignity of the disciplined heroic warrior.

With the systematic bombing of civilian populations, which began in Guernica in the Spanish Civil War, the distinctions between combatants and noncombatants and the tradition of chivalry have disappeared from warfare, leaving only the abstract virtue of obedience to duty. The warrior class in the modern state has increasingly been governed by an ethic that allows any atrocity in the name of "defense," an ethic that was spoken in classical form by Lieutenant Calley: "I will always put my duty to the American people above my personal conscience."

Chivalry is absent from modern warfare in part because technological advances in weapons make it difficult or impossible. A soldier with a bow or a rifle can distinguish clearly between a military and a civilian target. A bomber or fighter pilot strafing at high speeds can still make a fuzzy distinction between the guilty and the innocent. But nuclear weapons democratically incinerate all the enemy within a given territory. As Gen. S. L. A. Marshall noted,

Lawrence of Arabia
The Romantic Hero of W.W.1
James McBey. British Official War Artist, 1918

> The true objective not only of the atomic weapon but of rockets and modern bombing fleets is the physical destruction of a society. To suggest that these super-weapons should be aimed at military installations only would be like bringing up the heavy artillery to shoot at a clay pipe; they are designed, primarily, for no such limited target. . . . We see here . . . a curious transposition whereby the civilian mass becomes the shield covering the body of the military.[22]

Self-Portrait: Nazi as Hero
W.W. II

With the advent of nuclear missiles, the depth of the battlefield has been extended to include the entire world as well as outer space.

Politicians and some professional military still like to pretend that a nuclear "exchange" might be limited to manly blows between "hardened" missile sites in distant Wyoming or Siberia. But the notion of nuclear chivalry is nonsense. Instead of protecting civilians, the military is now hiding behind the skirts of women and children.

Without conventional arms and conventional wars the professional warrior cannot fight the kinds of battles he has been trained to fight. Some saw this early. Replacing war by omnicide means the warrior is spiritually unemployed. He can no longer demonstrate bravery, can no longer rescue his people from the enemy, can no longer shield the innocent behind himself, can no longer gain the immortality given to heroes. The nuclear weapon has castrated the heroic warrior, taken away his weapons, his field of battle, his honor.

THE ENEMY AS ABSTRACTION

The Final Insult

The execution of the Air-Land Battle doctrine will depend on our ability to distribute the information gained in microprocessors, embedded computers and data processing devices which are integral to the new system. The chip is the technological key to the new doctrine — the counterpart to the blitzkrieg's use of the gasoline engine.

Maj. Gen. John Woodmansee, Jr.

Modern technological warfare is gradually changing the way we think about the enemy. Both the heroic and the vitriolic images are being replaced by sterile concepts as the long reach of our weapons no longer makes it necessary for us to respect or hate those we intend to kill. The missile technician or the bomber pilot is so far removed from his "target" that he need not confront the carnage he inflicts. As one pilot who served in Vietnam told me, "I was OK so long as I was conducting high altitude missions, but when I had to come in and strafe and I could see the faces of the people I was killing, I got very disturbed." The ancient warrior needed massive physical strength and agility, a passionate hatred, and an ability to relish killing. He was either fierce, proud, arrogant, dominating, boastful, comfortable with cruelty, or dead. The modern warrior, by contrast, must be a specialist, coolheaded and emotionally detached. He prevails only if his calculations are accurate and his mind uncluttered by any passion save the love of efficiency. It has not escaped the attention of the

THE GREEDY ENEMY

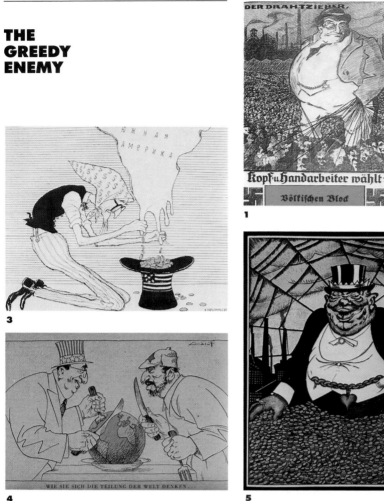

3

4

1

2

5

6

1. "The wirepuller. White-collar and manual workers vote for the folk ticket."—Germany, pre-W.W.II
2. Italy, W.W.II
3. U.S.S.R.   **4.** "How they see the division of the world."—Germany, W.W.II
5. The fat capitalist—U.S.S.R., 1930s   **6.** The U.S. promises dollars and work to the Italians, but if 12 million of its unemployed workers live on welfare, what will they be able to give to the conquered people except servitude and dishonor?"—Italy, W.W.II

THE
ENEMY
AS
CRIMINAL,
COMMITTER
OF
ATROCITIES,
TORTURER

1

2

3

4

5

6

1. The gangster—Italy, W.W.II **2.** Capitalist and militarist torturing the patriotic comrades—China, 1920s **3.** "Wanted: The Enemy of Humanity. Reward: Peace, Sobriety and Liberty."— Nicaragua, 1983 **4.** Atrocity stories charging German soldiers with cutting off the arms of women and children were widely circulated by the British press in W.W.I. Later investigation showed the charges to be without substance.

5. Vietnamese leader practicing to be Hitler—the archsadist—U.S.S.R. **6.** England, post-W.W.I

1

LADY MACBETH-BRITANNIA

2

„FORT! VERDAMMTER FLECK! FORT SAG ICH!" —
Shakespeare, „Macbeth" V. 1

3

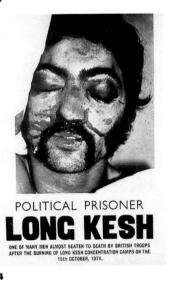

POLITICAL PRISONER
LONG KESH
ONE OF MANY MEN ALMOST BEATEN TO DEATH BY BRITISH TROOPS
AFTER THE BURNING OF LONG KESH CONCENTRATION CAMPS ON THE
15th OCTOBER, 1974.

4

USE OF CHEMICAL
WARFARE BY THE
IRAQI FORCES

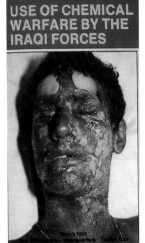

5

1. The U.S. accused of violating civil rights—U.S.S.R.
2. Lady Macbeth—Britain—Washing away the blood guilt for the bombing of civilians—Germany, W.W.II **3.** The Germans accused the Soviets of the massacre of Polish officers at Katyn. The Soviets accused the Germans. The controversy continues in present day Poland—France, W.W.II **4.** Ireland, I.R.A.
5. Iran, 1985

THE ENEMY AS RAPIST, DESECRATOR OF WOMEN AND CHILDREN

1

2

3

4

1. The beast, the barbarian, and the rapist themes are here combined in one image—U.S., W.W.I   **2.** "Here is how they warn white women in the U.S. about being assaulted by black gangsters. They are the same negroes that Roosevelt has invited to Italy . . ."—Italy, W.W.II   **3.** U.S., W.W.II   **4.** Note how pornographic bait is used to capture the attention of the viewer who, in turn, is expected to condemn the rapatious actions of the enemy—U.S., W.W.II

1

2

4

FRATELLI SALVATEMI!!
SOTTOSCRIVETE!

3

1. U.S.S.R., W.W.II **2.** The drowned mother and child refers to the German sinking of the Lusitania, a key factor in America's entrance into the war—U.S., W.W.I **3.** "Save me brother" (from the enemy).—Italy, W.W.II **4.** The enemy woman congratulates a pilot involved in terror bombing: "Charming, my dear! 5 churches, 1 restaurant, 2 hospitals, and how many children?"—Germany, W.W.II **5.** "The Family is the greatest infamy created in civil (capitalist) countries." Lenin—Italy, W.W.II **6.** U.S., W.W.II

5

6

SEX
AND
WAR

Propagandists portray absolute contrasts between us and them. Our soldiers love and respect women, who are pictured in the traditional heroic feminine roles of muse-inspirer, nurse, mother, companion, helpmate of the fighting man. Their soldiers are both rapists and desecrators of mothers and children. Should the enemy woman be presented she will be shown as victim or as the seducer who is sexually excited by brutality.

1

2

3

In Treue feft
Zur großen Rede des Führers über die Ereignisse des 30. Juni.

„Das deutsche Volk weiß: Je größer die Not, desto stärker immer der Führer!"
(Ministerpräsident Göring vor dem Reichstag am 13. Juli 1934.)

4

1. The Spirit (anima) of America—the innocent nurse **2.** The Seductive Spirit—she wants you to fight **3.** The Spirit of France—W.W.II **4.** The German Spirit. "The German People know, the greater the need, the greater the leader."

1

2

3

non tradite mio figlio

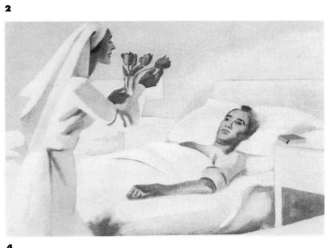

4

5

6

越南必胜！美国必败！

1. The Helpmate—Italy, W.W.II **2.** The Warrior's Mother: "Don't be a traitor to my son."—Italy, W.W.II **3.** The Italian Muse of War—W.W.II **4.** The Warrior's Nurse—Italy, W.W.II **5.** Companion in Arms—Italy, W.W.II **6.** "Vietnam must be saved, the United States must be resisted."—China

THE
ENEMY
AS
DEATH

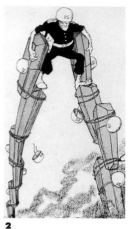

1. The U.S. as Death Incarnate—U.S.S.R.
2. Commentary on Vietnam—U.S.S.R. **3.** The communist threat—Germany, W.W.II **4.** "The foreign fascist hordes try to invade our territory. Antifascists! Let us block their way. Bury them forever in our soil."—Spanish Civil War **5.** The Enemy is chicken-footed Death—Nicaragua, wall mural

The uniform is a symptom of the mechanization of life, the emergence of mass mind, the submission to authority, the repression of conscience, the triumph of anonymity, the disease of abstraction.

We have become dominated in our thinking by a dangerous form of technicism *that leads Americans to view Vietnam (Vietnamization) as not more than a "job to be done" through the application of "American know-how."*
Robert Jay Lifton

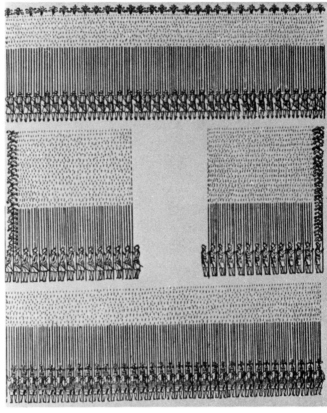

English Idealization of Greek Warfare

Army that the now and future warrior will have all the virtues of a computer expert and video game player.

The change from heroic tradition to modern warrior is from

Intimacy	to	Distance
Hot	to	Cool
Courage	to	Calculation
Hate	to	Feelinglessness
Physical fierceness	to	Intellectual accuracy
Individual initiative	to	Bureaucratic cooperation
Daring	to	Obedience

In the past when decisive victory was the point of war, a warrior needed to be aggressive, impatient, and ready for immediate action. Today stalling, posturing,

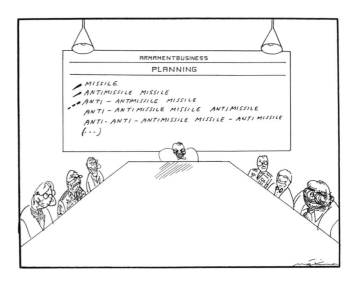

The Logic of Enmity
Maximo. Spain
© 1985 by Cartoonists and Writers Syndicate

rendering the threat of nuclear annihilation credible and creating stalemates is the essence of warfare. Hence another type of military personality is needed. The National War College has a course called "Executive Skills Development" that is directed at developing a personality called ISTJ (introverted, sensing, thinking, judging), and students are tested by using the Myers-Briggs Type Indicator, a test based on the work of Jung, that measures whether one is introverted or extroverted, intuitive or sensing, thinking or feeling, and judging or perceptive. The ISTJs like to look for canned answers, they want to know the right answer. This personality type is the same as the corporate executive—objective decision makers. According to psychologist Otto Kroeger, a consultant to the U.S. Army,

> This corporate personality is something fairly new in the military, and it helps explain why during war games, the students prefer deterrence to destruction. The peacetime Army does not have the George Patton type. They've been weeded out. I know a number who have early-outed in the last ten years. The action types, the hard-nosed risk-taking daredevils, said, "I didn't come to push papers. I joined the action Army and there's no action."[23]

As the modern warrior has become increasingly disembodied and warfare an intellectual and technological matter, the enemy has been progressively reduced to an abstraction.

82

The process began with the introduction of the drum and the uniform. Forcing men to march to a single cadence and to dress in ways that eradicated all distinctions, removed the element of individuality that was essential to heroic warfare. Enemies and allies alike are all pretty much olive drab or dull gray. Like a unit in a society governed by mass production, the soldier has been reduced to standardized functionary. He is a part of a well-oiled war machine, and his highest virtue is to function efficiently, which involves obeying the orders of his superiors. And the enemy is merely an impediment, an obstacle to be removed.

Occasionally we use machine images to dehumanize the enemy. We suggest that he is an automaton, a mindless being who is programmed by some higher, but demonic, intelligence. The enemy as automaton is an updated version of the enemy as puppet. In both cases what is central is the notion that he has no independent will and is controlled by something beyond himself. Hence we should have no more compunction in dispatching him than we would in destroying a robot. There is no soul in the machine.

More often than lending the enemy even the slight dignity we accord to machines, we simply erase him from our field of vision and act as if he is not there. Robert Bathurst reports that in the 1970s the U.S. Naval War College got the idea "that the study of war can be abstracted from people." After Vietnam there was a feeling that the language of war and enemies was immoral and old-fashioned, and that these subjects

"The Threat: Theirs is Bigger Than Ours"
U.S. Defense Department, 1985

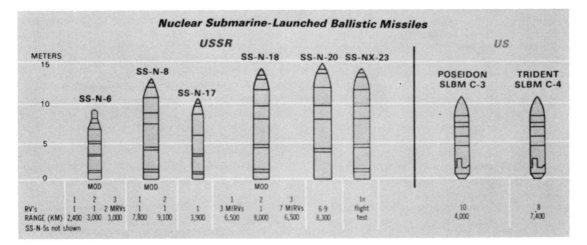

Nuclear Submarine-Launched Ballistic Missiles

USSR — US

SS-N-6, SS-N-8, SS-N-17, SS-N-18, SS-N-20, SS-NX-23, POSEIDON SLBM C-3, TRIDENT SLBM C-4

METERS: 15, 10, 5, 0

	SS-N-6			SS-N-8		SS-N-17	SS-N-18			SS-N-20	SS-NX-23	POSEIDON SLBM C-3	TRIDENT SLBM C-4
		MOD			MOD			MOD					
RV's	1	2	3 2 MRVs	1	2	1	1 3 MIRVs	2	3 7 MIRVs	6-9	In flight test	10	8
RANGE (KM)	2,400	3,000	3,000	7,800	9,100	3,900	6,500	8,000	6,500	8,300		4,000	7,400

SS-N-5s not shown

83

could be made more agreeable by being denationalized and universalized. Thus all specific references to the Soviets as enemies were deleted from textbooks, and men were told that they would be fighting to defend "land areas." "With such planning armed forces tend to become transformed into enormous riot squads being sent to a neighborhood they don't know to fight an enemy difficult to recognize, an enemy with technological characteristics, but no human face."[24]

Nowhere has the statistical, abstract concept of the enemy become more obvious than in the American practice in Vietnam of determining "progress" in war by announcing daily "body counts." Under such conditions all it took to define an enemy was a body. As the popular saying went, "If it's dead, it's Viet Cong." The enemy is only a number used in our mathematical calculations. He is one of 6 million Jews killed, 20 million Soviets, 8,000 Sandinistas, 36 Arab terrorists, 250,000 Hindus, and so forth.

One professional soldier with much combat experience, Col. Anthony Herbert, translates the pathetic language of abstraction into its tragic reality:

> To say that it had not been a very important day because the Second Battalion had but two NVA kills now seems ludicrous; it was a damned important day for those two dead men. When even just one man died or got his fingers blown off or his leg shattered or his hearing impaired or his eyes bloodied and blinded, it was one hell of a costly battle — especially if you happened to be the guy who got it that day. It's something generals and presidents can never understand — only mothers, fathers, brothers, sons and daughters, and wives. . . . If anything has happened to our country as a result of the Vietnam War, it is our national infection with the sickness of the numbers game. We reduced the blood and suffering and the death and destruction to mere ciphers, and in so doing we reduced our own souls. Numbers don't die; people do. Columns of figures don't disintegrate in the explosion of a bomb; human beings do. Statistics don't bleed, and if you can make your war a war of numbers, you have no trouble sleeping. Most generals and presidents sleep well.[25]

The old metaphors of devil and beast still inhabit our political language, especially when we are characterizing more "primitive," "Third World" enemies such

Statistics 101

Look out for No. 1.
Only body counts.

I + Thou is more than 2.
Soul Counts.

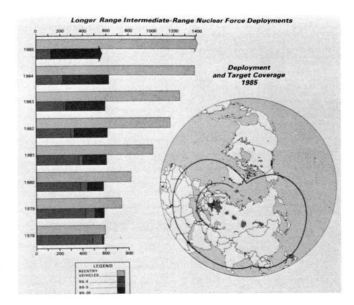

Longer Range Intermediate-Range Nuclear Force Deployments

Deployment and Target Coverage 1985

The World as Target
U.S. Defense Department, 1985

as Khadafy or Khomeini. But in the major conflict between the United States and the Soviet Union the most prevalent visual images we use do not portray any person, demon, or beast but the actual weapons system of the enemy. The hostile imagination has become modernized. Just as *Time* magazine announced a couple of years ago that "the man of the year" was a computer, so the enemy of the year is the current military technology of the other side. The American is the Pershing Missile; the Soviet is the SS20. In portraying what we both call "*the* threat," both the United States and the Soviets picture each others' military hardware—tanks, rockets, bombers, fighters, missiles. We exhibit elaborate graphs and quote statistics about comparative firepower and destructive capacity, and argue about whose weapons are first strike and whose are defensive. It is as if people had vanished from the scene and we expected the next war to be fought between weapon systems that were directed by preprogrammed computer scenarios. And indeed, this horrific vision of an automated, impersonal war becomes increasingly probable as our computers become more sensitive and our weapons more ultrasonic. We stand in danger of an accidental apocalypse triggered by computers that are programmed to launch on warning.

On a smaller scale the "automated battlefield" of the future in which machines (for the technologically elite nations) replace men has already arrived. In the later days of the Vietnam war

> on the Ho Chi Minh Trail in Laos there has been a project known as "Igloo White" in which acoustic and seismic sensors—devices highly sensitive to sound and vibrations—have been placed in long spears flung from high-speed aircraft and stuck into the ground in a series. The radio-connected microphones, dropped near the spears by parachute, record information from the sensors and transmit it to a surveillance plane flying in the area. . . . After being fed into a computer, the information is evaluated by "skilled target analysts" who decide whether it suggests enemy forces, friendly troops, trucks, animals, or whatnot. If the decision is enemy troops, an air strike is set in motion. . . . The only awareness of "the enemy" comes from electronic feedback in the form of "blips" on a screen.[26]

Lifton goes on to comment that this final reduction of the enemy to a blip does not even require the electronic warrior to go through the psychological process of reducing the enemy to a "gook"—a dirty, slimy, death-tainted object who could be brutalized or killed without guilt. The atrocities committed from a high altitude by bomber crews, directed from afar by technicians are not so much inhumane as ahuman. The numbed warrior does not need to dehumanize his enemy because he has never had any emotional involvement with his victims.

To see how completely we have dehumanized and eliminated the enemy, even to the point of not dignifying him with an image we can hate, we must look at the euphemistic language of modern warfare. Our weapons have become so indiscriminate and omnicidal that we dare not look specifically at the enemy on whom they will fall. To imagine what nuclear weapons will do would require the "nice" technician, the computer specialist, the games theorist, the modern human general, to admit that he is contemplating a crime against humanity that makes Hitler's extermination camps appear small scale. To visualize the millions of Soviet or American men, women, and children who would be incinerated by even a small atomic "device" might upset our digestion. So long as we want to kill from a distance with clean hands, we must refrain from imagining the consequences of our weapons, and must

Doonesbury, by Garry Trudeau.
Copyright, 1972, G. B. Trudeau.
Reprinted with permission. All
rights reserved.

*This "objective" attitude — talking
about concentration camps in terms
of "administration," and about
extermination camps in terms of
"economy"—was typical of the S.S.
mentality, and something Eichmann, at the trial, was still very
proud of.*
Hannah Arendt

completely eliminate any awareness of the enemy as
human. Our new language of warfare is not accidental.
The Air Force colonel who described the Titan II missile with a nine-megaton warhead as "a potentially dis-
ruptive re-entry system" (and was awarded the National
Association of English Teacher's American Doublespeak
Award in 1983), should have also gotten the Adolph
Eichmann Memorial Prize. When a missle warhead
becomes a "re-entry vehicle," when killing civilians
becomes "collateral damage," when the destruction of
cities becomes "counter-value," when an MX missile
becomes "Peacemaker," when combat becomes "violence processing," when destroying entire areas with
Agent Orange becomes "an environmental adjustment,"
and peace becomes "permanent pre-hostility," we have
reached the end of the line of dehumanization: 100 on
a scale of 100. (Incidentally, the Grenada "invasion"
was changed by the U.S. State Department first to a
"rescue mission" and then to "a pre-dawn vertical inser-
tion.") When the warrior makes only technical decisions
with no reference to moral considerations, the enemy is
reduced to a cipher, a statistical unit. Both the warrior
and the enemy have disappeared. No living, feeling,
agonizing, tragic, cruel, compassionate, courageous,
fearful, anxious person is left on the battlefield, which
has now become the entire world. Only machines fighting other machines. Little wonder that when Army
futurists speculate about the human aspects of Airland
Battle 2000 they present us with the ultimate triumph
and nemesis of the historical union of *Homo faber* and
Homo hostilis:

> The human aspects of Airland Battle 2000 are of
> genuine concern for which we have far more ques-

87

tions than answers. Will soldiers be able to exist on
the battlefield of the year 2000? Or are we imagining such a technologically hostile environment that
soldiers themselves will not be accommodated? We
expect, in addition to more and worse physical
wounds, more psychological stress casualties.
Whole battle staffs of professional officers may collapse; commanders may have to be replaced or dual
command instituted. Human engineering to immunize our soldiers against stress may be required,
just as we now immunize against disease.[27]

When war has become so terrible that we can no
longer bear to think about those we destroy and when
we must think of "engineering" a new breed of man to
withstand the horror, it should be clear that *Homo
hostilis* has reached the end of the line.

We are faced with choices so radical that any one of
them will completely change the way we think about
ourselves. We may resign from all hope of remaining
human and alive and accept our fate as anonymous victims of "potentially dangerous re-entry systems." If we
refuse this path of impotent despair, we may control
our technology, run the arms race backward, and learn
to fight limited wars with minimal weapons. Or we may
undertake the heroic psychological, political, and spiritual task of transforming our ancient habit of enmity.

Total War
Germany, W.W. II

**Hiroshima: The Enemy
Vanquished; The Triumph of
Abstraction**

PART 2

THE PSYCHOLOGY OF ENMITY

We have met the enemy, and he is us.
Pogo (Walt Kelly)

Our life-giving, "Bio-Philic" half has a hostile, "Necro-Philic" side.
Robert Osborn. From *Mankind May Never Make It!* New York Graphic Society. Used by permission.

The era of modern, total war is nearly finished. We are living in the last days in which men can live by the sword without humankind perishing by the bomb. The warrior psyche, which has thus far governed what we insist on calling the history of civilization, has brought us to the point of suicide, if not cosmocide. Either we awake from the nightmare of violence or we sleepwalk into oblivion. And likely there will be no fire, during the long nuclear winter, and no storyteller left to remember that our generals and statesmen were leaders of a race of lemmings that was endowed with a promise of reason and a potentiality for compassion that might have made us human beings.

It is rapidly becoming obvious that the "realistic" ways in which we think about warfare and enemies are morally and intellectually bankrupt, delusional, and self-destructive. To date, warfare has been considered, as Clausewitz summarized it, "a continuation of politics by other means." And peace has been, for the most part, polite warfare in slow motion. Politics and warfare have served a common end of tribal and national conquest. And the warrior psyche has maintained its dominance not only by arms and threat of violence, but by cultivating the unshakeable illusion that "the enemy" is an objective fact of the exterior world.

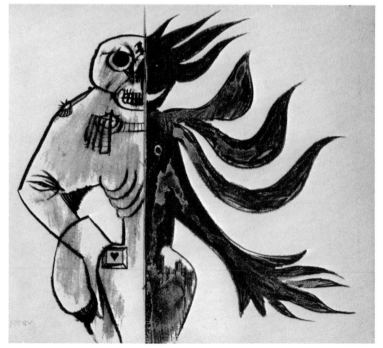

*Madness is something rare in
individuals—but in groups, parties,
peoples, ages, it is the rule.*
Nietszche

Realistically, most of what has masqueraded as practical politics and rational warfare has been mass madness, corporate schizophrenia. Rarely is warfare an effective solution to conflict. Therefore we will fall far short of investigating promising solutions to the problem of war if we limit ourselves to looking for rational, exterior, political means for adjudicating conflict. No doubt, the habit of warfare will not be ended without an effective international law and enforcement agency and the creation of new political institutions both within and between nations. But even less will it be ended without a psychological transformation of large numbers of individuals.

In the final part of this book—"The Future of Enmity"—I will suggest some of the institutional changes we must make to end the era of *Homo hostilis* and wean ourselves from the war system. In this part I will look at the psychology of enmity, and begin the task of demythologizing the enemy, reowning our projections, making conscious the unconscious of the body politic, ending the tyranny of the extroverts, a tyranny in which psychological events have been politicized and the unacknowledged fears of power-obsessed men have been the hidden motive force of what has passed as the "real" world of politics.

FROM VICTIM TO AGENT

On Reowning Responsibility

Healing begins when we cease playing the blame game, when we stop assigning responsibility for war to some mysterious external agency and dare to become conscious of our violent ways.

The major responsibility for war lies not with villains and evil men but with reasonably good citizens. Any depth understanding of the social function of war leads to the conclusion that it was the "good" Germans who created the social ecology that nurtured the Nazis, just as it was the "good" Americans, working through their warrior priests such as General Westmoreland, who sent Lieutenant Calley into MyLai. Lincoln said, "War is much too important to be left to the generals." But the psychological truth is much more disturbing. The generals are the (largely unconscious) agents of a (largely unconscious) civilian population. The good people send out armies as the symbolic representatives to act out their repressed shadows, denied hostilities,

America as Policeman
Louis Dalrymple. 1905

We become what we hate.

unspoken cruelties, unacceptable greed, unimagined lust for revenge against punitive parents and authorities, uncivil sexual sadism, denied animality, in a purifying blood ritual that confirms their claim to goodness before the approving eyes of history or God. Warfare is the political equivalent of the individual process of seeking "vindictive triumph," which Karen Horney described as the essence of neurosis.

The persistent efforts of liberals, peacemongers, and assorted groups of nice people to assign the blame for war to the Pentagon, the military-industrial complex, or some other surrogate for the devil, are no less a denial of responsibility than laying the blame on an external enemy. The sentimental cliché "The people don't want war, only their leaders do," is a pious way to avoid thinking seriously about the problem. And we will not make progress in severing the roots of war without re-owning our consensual paranoia and the corporate responsibility for evil. The body politic will change only when there is a democratization of guilt, responsibility, power, and authority. We become politically potent by accepting responsibility, for better or worse, for the conduct of our leaders. In the long view, nations have the leaders they deserve.

What is necessary is not an easy confession, but a political work, a path, a discipline of consciousness that must be undertaken by a community of solitary individuals. There is no way to repent *en masse*. The burden of corporate guilt can only be borne by individuals sensitive enough to examine their own consciousness and conscience. This is the way of metanoia, changing our minds, reversing our perspectives, making conscious the projections of our shadows onto the enemy.

America as Hypocrite
Joseph Keppler. 1891

OUR ENEMIES MAKE NERVE GAS. SO WILL WE.

THEY SQUANDER THEIR WEALTH ON ARMAMENTS. SO WILL WE.

THEY SPY ON THEIR OWN CITIZENS. SO WILL WE.

THEY PREVENT THEIR PEOPLE FROM KNOWING WHAT THEY DO. SO WILL WE.

SECRET

WE WILL NOT LET OUR ENEMIES IMPOSE THEIR EVIL WAYS ON US.

WE'LL DO IT FOR THEM.

STEIN '83
ROCKY MTN. NEWS • NEA

Our enemies
Ed Stein. Rocky Mt. News

If we desire peace, each of us must begin to demythologize the enemy; cease politicizing psychological events; re-own our shadows; make an intricate study of the myriad ways in which we disown, deny, and project our selfishness, cruelty, greed, and so on onto others; be conscious of how we have unconsciously created a warrior psyche and have perpetuated warfare in its many modes:

1. *The civil war within the self*—the enemy within, agonizing self-consciousness, the struggle between "I should" and "I want," the battle between "good" and "evil" parts of the self

2. *The war between the sexes*—combat in the erogenous zones, the creation of familiar enemies, the practice of seduction, rape, one-upmanship. The sadistic-masochistic element in sexual and familiar relationships, the practice of superiority-inferiority, winners and victims

3. *The political war between Us and Them*—how our psyches have been shaped by the consensual paranoia and the standard propaganda of our society and by the barrage of images of the enemy

4. *The battle against nature, life*—the measure in which we have a propensity to identify ourselves "against," to assume that we must struggle, control, dominate, in order to be safe; the mistrust of self, others, life.

It should go without saying that individuals dealing with their personal enmity will not automatically solve the problem of warfare. But it is likewise certain that the politics of the warrior will not change without a constituency of individuals who have made the solitary

"We'll dress him up differently,
but his content suits us fine!"

Soviet View of U.S.
Post-W.W.II

decision to follow the path of metanoia rather than paranoia and to begin the practice of compassion rather than competition. Or, as the matter was stated a long time ago, "Remove first the beam from your own eye and then you will see more clearly to remove the mote from your brother's eye."

I believe the initiative for world peace at this time in history rests primarily with North Americans. Our repentance will be the major factor in determining the future of enmity. To use an analogy, every family therapist knows that the healthiest person in a diseased family system bears the most responsibility for changing the conflict and pathology of the system. For various historical reasons, the Soviet Union is an exceptionally paranoid nation. The United States is slightly less paranoid. Therefore, we have a greater responsibility to introduce sanity, to be willing to repent of our mistakes, to de-escalate our propaganda, to demythologize the "communist" as enemy. Our blame for world conflict is not greater, but our psychological opportunity for resolution is greater. When it comes to the individual task of reowning the enemy, of practicing metanoia, we are all equal. The journey into the wilderness of the shadow requires a heroic and solitary effort of anyone who would make it. But Americans, at least, have a wide access to alternative media, to information, and therapeutic help which is necessary to become genuinely self-critical, to jump outside the prison of the tribal or national psyche.

THE ENEMY AS MIRROR

Propaganda as Disowned Truths

When I was a child and I pointed my finger in blame at my brother, my mother always said, "Remember, when you point your finger at somebody, three fingers are pointing back at you." Blaming, "projection" as psychologists call it, is learned early and remains a primitive defense mechanism, a way by which we magically split the self and claim the good for ourselves and disown all that our parents consider bad. The stronger the habit of blame, the greater the split between the conscious image of the "good" self and the unconscious feelings of the "bad" self and the more enemies we create to bear the burden of our rejected self.

When we reach the point in the journey of the human spirit where we want to become conscious, we must be willing to become real rather than "good." Our greatest resource, then, is to conquer the psychological territory we have previously ceded to the enemy. The images of the enemy are the mirror in which we can see our yet-unknown self. If, as Freud said, the dream is the royal road to the unconscious, the image of the enemy—the dream of the body politic—is the royal road to the collective unconscious. "Love your enemy as yourself" is not so much a perfectionistic moral injunction as it is a revelation of the only possible path toward self-knowledge and self-acceptance.

The first rule for discovering the treasure hidden in images of the enemy is this: Listen to what the enemy says about you, and you will learn the truth you have repressed. To come to greater self-understanding, borrow the eyes of the alien, see yourself from afar. Let the familiar become strange and the strange familiar—the two rules of creativity. Look with suspicion on the rhetoric of your nation and listen with compassion to the reasons of the enemy. Apple basket turnover. Repent. Change perspectives. Give your eye (your *I*) a vacation. Try on a different head. Turn your paranoia inside out; practice metanoia.

We will begin to end warfare not when we have better weapons, but when we speak truer words. The link between lying and violence, propaganda and war, has long been recognized. Speaking of the Civil War in Corcyra 427 B.C., Thucydides said, in *The Peloponnesian Wars*,

> To fit in with the change in events, words, too, had to change their usual meanings. What used to be described as a thoughtless act of aggression was now regarded as the courage one would expect to find in a party member; to think of the future and wait was merely another way of saying one was a coward; any idea of moderation was just an attempt to disguise one's unmanly character; ability to understand a question from all sides meant that one was totally unfitted for action. Fanatical enthusiasm was the mark of a real man, and to plot against an enemy behind his back was perfectly legitimate self-defense. Anyone who held violent opinions could always be trusted, and anyone who objected to them became suspect. To plot successfully was a sign of intelligence, but it was still cleverer to see that a plot was hatching. If one attempted to provide against having to do either, one

The U.S. Seen Through Viet Cong Eyes

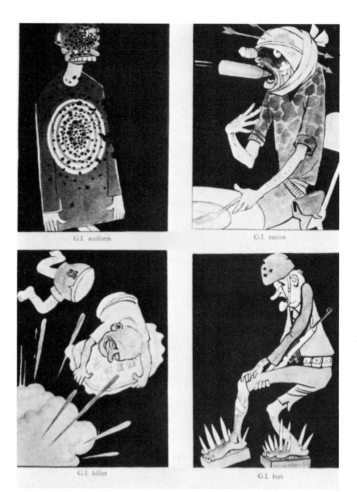

G.I. uniform   G.I. ration

G.I. billet   G.I. feet

The enemy, a Viet Cong view

was disrupting the unity of the party and acting out of fear of the opposition. In short, it was equally praiseworthy to get one's blow in first against someone who was going to do wrong, and to denounce someone who had no intention of doing wrong at all. Family relations were a weaker tie than party membership since party members were more ready to go to any extreme for any reason whatever.

Confucius claimed we could have harmony in society if we named things accurately. Peace begins with the rectification of terms. Somehow we missed the obvious meaning of the myth of Genesis. When God linked human dignity to the task of naming the animals, the point was not that human beings were supposed to lord

I am the State. We are the State.
U.S.S.R.

I shall always be guilty so long as I belong to a nation at all. Yet there is no good life apart from some nation or other.
Glenn Gray

it over everybody. We were intended to be poets, not conquistadors. The human essence, the soul, the self, is revealed not in the schizophrenic psyche of the warrior, but in the healing naming and chanting of the poet. We lose our essence when we fall into propaganda—false naming. We exile ourselves from the garden of the spirit when we pervert language and give a false sanctity to acts of destruction. Changing vices into virtues, we become inhumane.

> Over the expanse of five continents throughout the coming years an endless struggle is going to be pursued between violence and friendly persuasion. . . . Henceforth the only honorable course will be to stake everything on a formidable gamble; that words are more powerful than munitions.
>
> Albert Camus

We may begin healing our diseased species by a small but radical reclaiming of language, by ceasing to sanctify blind obedience to authority with the honorific "duty," or call the willingness to kill an unknown enemy or die in the attempt "courage," or baptize the spirit of revenge with the name of "honor." The word *hero* needs to be reserved for the man or woman who is willing to take the solitary journey into the depths of the self, to reown the shadow, to exorcise the ancient warrior psyche, to discover the power and authority of wholeness. And the word *courage* should be reserved to characterize the man or woman who leaves the infantile sanctuary of the mass mind, to live in the creative anxiety of meditative and reflective consciousness. And *duty* can be nothing less than the refusal to allow a national consensus of communal narcissism to displace the "transmoral conscience" that is the true human instinct for universal compassion.

THE GRAMMAR OF METANOIA

How to Repent and Love Your Enemy-Self

Repentance is for little children.
Adolf Eichmann

Unless you become as a little child you will not enter into the kingdom of heaven.
Jesus

In theory, metanoia is simple, in practice, agonizing. The method of conciliation, the discipline of compassion, leads through the heart of darkness: begin with the projection, the image of the enemy, and return to the self. Reverse the direction of the current. Introjection rather than projection. Guilt rather than blame. Leave heaven to angels and politicians and descend into hell. Make friends with the devil.

The method: Change your pronouns. In matters of politics, change from *they* to *we* to *I*, from disowned guilt and responsibility to corporate-authority-guilt-responsibility, to individual potency-guilt-responsibility. In matters of interpersonal relationships, change from *you* to *I-thou* from the habit of infantile blame and omnipotent expectation to mature interdependence and mutuality. In matters of relationships between ego and self, change from *it* to *I*, from denial of the dehumanizing parts of the self that are despised to acceptance of the plurality of the self.

On this path there are no objective experts, only repentant warriors and wounded lovers. The exploration of the psychology of enmity that follows is offered in the spirit of tentative analysis and confession. It is at best a series of suggestions of how we may demythologize the enemy, a small contribution to the task that must be the major human vocation of our time—the understanding of the symbolism, politics, psychology of enmity and friendship.

PARANOIA REVISITED

On Being Against

The consensual paranoia that ordinarily erupts politically as warfare is rooted in the perennial struggle within the psyche between basic trust and mistrust. In varying degrees, we all have the disposition to be paranoid or trusting. Karen Horney says in *Neurosis and Human Growth*, in principle we can move *toward*, *against*, or *away from* others. Healthy people retain the ability to do all three; neurotics specialize in one. To the degree that a child is raised by neurotic parents, the child does not develop a feeling of belonging, of "we," but instead a profound insecurity and vague apprehensiveness, for which Horney uses the term *basic anxiety*—a feeling of being isolated and helpless in a world conceived as potentially hostile. We need only add that a majority of the world's children have been raised by parents who were crippled in their ability to love, both by the unconscious paranoia of their societies and by

The Dollar Bacillus causes, (1) a paroxysm of rage among the warmongers, (2) fits and hallucinations among the Hearstlings, (3) armament fever, (4) a crisis from which the patient will not recover.
U.S.S.R.

KEEP PERSHING II AND CRUISE MISSILE OUT OF EUROPE!

International Union of Students

The principles of war—maneuver, objective, offensive surprise, economy of force, unity of command, simplicity and security—are good guides to running competitive business.
William Peacock

their own individual neurotic injuries. What psychology has recently called *neurosis*, and acknowledged to be near universal, theologians once called *sin*, *estrangement*, or *alienation*. The word *paranoia* is only the most recent name for this perennial human temptation to yield to a pervasive need of radical mistrust, defensiveness, and cynicism.

As a mode of perception that often becomes a style of life, paranoia weaves around the vulnerable self or group an air-tight metaphysic and world view. Paranoia is an antireligious mysticism based on the feeling or perception that the world in general, and others in particular, are *against* me or us. Reality is perceived as hostile. By contrast, the religious mystic experiences the ground of being as basically friendly to the deepest needs of the self. That which is unknown, strange, and beyond our comprehension is *with* and *for* rather than *against* us. Evil may be penultimately powerful, but goodness, as William James said, "casts the last stone." In religious language, this stance is symbolized by the affirmation that God is Love. The paranoid individual or community operates on the supposition that what is strange is aligned in a hostile conspiracy against us. A single network of malevolent intent stretches over the world. "They" are out to get us. As the religious mystic turns to and trusts in God or the ground of being, the paranoid mystic organizes life around combat against the enemy.

The best way to ferret out hidden paranoia is to listen carefully to words and metaphors. The vocabulary of paranoia is organized around the words *war, battle, strategy, tactics, struggle, contest, competition, winning, enemies, opponents, they, defenses, security, maneuver, objective, power, command, control, willpower, assault.* Heraclitus, the pre-Socratic philosopher, gave the first philosophical expression of the paranoid world view: "War is the father of all things." Hobbes later applied the insight to human conduct and concluded that in a state of nature men were all enemies to each other—wolves. Sartre carried it a step further and concluded that when two people look at each other there is an inevitable battle in which each tries to appropriate the subjectivity of the other: "Hell is other people." In modern times, paranoia has mostly clothed itself in economic and political rhetoric. In the communist world the rhetoric is dialectical materialism, the perception of history as the story of a clash between rival classes. In capitalism it is the myth of competition

Paranoia, American Style
Dale Cummings. Canada
© 1985 by Cartoonists and Writers Syndicate

in which individual selfishness is somehow supposed to add up to the common good. Both communism and capitalism agree that warfare is the organizing metaphor. They disagree only about whether the holy war (the war to end wars) is the international class conflict or "peaceful" competition between multinational corporations. In business-oriented societies, executives (those who execute) "make a killing" by beating the competition, getting to the top of the heap, staying ahead. In recent times this campaign has involved tactics familiar to any general: intelligence gathering, industrial spies, bribes. Among the most popular literature for those who are looking out for No. 1 are a legion of books on how to get and use power, power dressing, the craft of power, power foods (not quiche), and so on. Even when we turn to dealing with other social problems we think primarily in terms of warfare: the war against poverty, the war against hunger, the war against cancer. It does not occur to the paranoid mind that perhaps warfare and defense and "attacking" problems are not the most hopeful metaphors to use in thinking about perennial human suffering.

Most of us who are reasonably good people experience our paranoia, if at all, in garden-variety ways. We might all recite the normal citizen's version of the Paranoid's Confession:

I realize that I do not trust other people very much. When I begin to peel the onion of my personality, I encounter layer after layer of delusion, illusion, pretense, rationalization, postures, prepared dialogues, covert motives, false modesty, disguised egotism, strategies for establishing my superiority, tactics for putting down others, mechanisms of denial, projection, overcompensation. My mind appears to me, at times, to be an intricate defense establishment. My explanation, theories, ideas, protect me against a jumble of feelings. My cleverness, well-timed puns, jokes, wisecracks, quick wit, allow me to stay in control of social situations and prevent me from getting close to people.

I am filled with prejudices against people different from myself. I don't entirely trust that alien species that inhabits half the planet—the opposite sex—otherwise why would I try so hard to please them and stay in control at the same time. And as far as that is concerned, I don't trust members of my own sex very much. I guard myself against vulnerability and self-disclosure, keep a safe distance. I cultivate my image, polish my role, prac-

The Greatest Soviet fear
U.S.S.R.

"We must be on our guard with those Russians—they are literally charging into battle, firing one peace proposal after another at our heads!"
U.S.S.R. views U.S. as phobic about peace
U.S.S.R.

tice my profession, attain the marks of status, protect my self-esteem in a thousand small ways, as if other people were constantly trying to make me less than I am. My ego is a kind of sensitive enclosure that has a constantly active distant-early-warning system, that alerts me against dangers to my self-esteem. I have a friend or two whom I let get close, but I take care to keep the key of my fortress in my own keeping.

I work hard to provide for my security and worry a lot about the future. When I dare to look closely I find some unnameable fear, suspicion, mistrust, lurking around anything where I have to yield control of my mind or body. I don't allow my imagination full play because I don't entirely trust what images will emerge when I am not censuring myself. "To sleep, perchance to dream." Sometimes I find myself unexpectedly thinking violent thoughts, imagining I have an antitank weapon and blow the son-of-a-bitch who just cut me off in traffic off the road. Or even that I kill someone who has just insulted me.

On those rare occasions when I allow myself to think about death, The Terror rises from the pit of my stomach to my throat. How can the universe be designed so that I am to be eradicated? The thought fills me with anger, rage, defiance. And then I get back to work, polishing a project that will create a sea wall against the tide of death. I secretly feel a mixture of grief and relief when someone I know dies, because I am still alive. Thus far I have escaped; therefore I must be special; perhaps even immune to mortality. I know it's not rational.

I don't have a lot of enemies; don't believe the propaganda about the unique evil of communism. Oh, I know they are a lot worse than we are, but still we have enough faults not to be always throwing stones. But I have a number of domestic enemies, men, mostly, who I think are in the service of an evil delusion. I tend to vilify the Pentagon only slightly less than the Kremlin, not to trust the very rich or the very poor, the lazy or the outrageously sexy. Make mine moderate. I do fight from time to time with my spouse. And there can be no question in any reasonable person's mind that I am not to blame. Sometimes we get locked into a vicious circle of attack and reprisal that leaves us both exhausted and wondering how we can create so much enmity in the closure of intimacy. I live and let live, but when my neighbor trespasses over my boundary, I am coiled and ready to strike. Don't tread on me. In fact I

New Year's Gift by the Pentagon: Western Europe
U.S.S.R.

am jealous of whatever power, possessions, and prestige I have managed to accumulate and will defend when threatened. I believe I should love my neighbor, even strangers, and I do practice charity in moderation so long as my space is not invaded.

I have nightmares peopled with violent men and women, terrorists who attack my fortress, but I have never killed or even struck another person in anger. I do enjoy a few murders daily on TV and a little ritualized violence in the NFL. I have some perverse tendency I cannot understand: my eye catches first in the newspaper the passage about rape, murder, torture. It is almost as if I relish the violence that I simultaneously deplore. I contribute to Amnesty International and am fascinated and repulsed by their tales of torture. Yet never have I bruised the flesh of another human being. Nor will, if I can help it.

I know my faults. I accuse myself before you are able and thereby blunt any possible criticism that can be made against me. I maintain a good opinion of myself even when it takes a lot of inner dialogue to convince me to believe my own press clippings. My first impulse is to judge others but try to understand myself. I have a long memory for slights and insults to my being, and although I will forgive, I usually require some signs of repentance. Say you're sorry, and I will be magnanimous.

I know there is evil in the world and more than that, immense tragedy; from genocide in Cambodia to famine in Ethiopia. And it tugs at my heartstrings when I see war-torn lands and hungry children. But in truth I still eat hearty each day and pacify my conscience with slight charity.

Mostly I avoid situations where violence threatens. I feel those who deal in arms and blood, cops and generals, are somehow contaminated, even when they are doing dirty work that keeps me safe. If some incarnation of evil as unambiguous as Hitler appeared again, I would have no moral qualms about killing the enemy. But in the modern world of moral murkiness, I prefer to keep my hands as clean of enemy blood as possible. Perhaps that allows me to preserve an easy innocence, to make a separate peace, to evade some of the moral agony of a world gone mad with nuclear technology. So be it.

We are all larger and smaller than we pretend to be in normal life. Like Alice, we are always expanding and

Truman and MacArthur Scheming
China

Uncle Sam Cheering for Himself
Roger. Nicaragua
© 1985 by Cartoonists and Writers Syndicate

shrinking. Although our "realistic" ego image of ourselves is more or less tailored to our accomplishments and the feedback we get, our unconscious "neurotic" image of self oscillates between omnipotent and impotent views, expectations, and feelings about ourselves. We constantly devise strategies for proving we are superior to others, and to the degree that we are successful we almost immediately find some way to compensate for our unconscious feelings of inferiority. To confess our inferiority, we fail, get sick, worry, get depressed. In the healthy self, these two extremes gradually become conscious. We become aware of our projections of superiority and inferiority, our judgmentalness, put-ups and put-downs, and become more realistic in our assessment of ourself and others. We gradually leave behind the infantile stance where we were in relationship to omnipotent parents in whose presence we felt small.

The neurotic, Everyman as child, perceives the world as made up of big and little people, those with power and those who are impotent, tops and bottoms, victors and victims. In this world view there is no place for equality. One's position in the up-down game may change, but the game goes on because it allows both partners to live in the illusion that somebody is in charge. Even if I must play the childish victim role, it is comforting to know there are powerful adults around who, if they punish me, will also protect me.

On the level of propaganda, it is easy to see this swing reflected in our perceptions of the enemy. At one moment he is a giant whose overwhelming strength is threatening to annihilate us; at the next he is a diminutive creature, subhuman and worthless, to be eliminated, a nuisance rather than a threat.

The only way out is to stop the game. Be neither one up nor one down. Liberty, equality, fraternity, sorority. Only conflicts between people of the same size, or nations of the same dignity, can be solved in a reasonable way. The rule of law is established by mutually honoring the fundamental assumption that all men, women, children, and possibly other sentient beings are equal. The very existence of justice and law is predicated on the intention of people and communities (and eventually sovereign nations) to play the equality game.

FUNCTIONAL ATHEISM

The Ego in Narcissism and Nationalism

Narcissism is microatheism.
Nationalism is macroatheism.

The charge that the enemy is an atheist rests on a level of thought so superficial it will not withstand the slightest critical analysis. The theology of the tribe and the nation-state is composed of equal parts of propaganda directed against an enemy and pious self-image management for domestic consumption. Both numb the faculties of thought, imagination, and feeling.

If we put aside ideological and political definitions of atheism as "the worship of gods other than those we worship," the haunting and perennial existential question that determines how we organize our lives is: do I seek to make myself the center of the world, the *raison d'être* for all that is around me, or do I seek to be a harmonious part of some mysterious totality that transcends my individuality? Functionally speaking, atheism is narcissism—the ego's refusal of transcendence, the decision to reduce other people and nonhuman life to means that serve the end of increasing the power, pleasure, and security of the ego. Nationalism is mass narcissism, the decision of the body politic to make other nations serve as means of increasing the power and security of the nation.

In mass societies, atheism is scarcely ever manifest as a formal denial of God. And where atheism is an official governmental policy, as in the U.S.S.R., the state makes itself a divinity. Functionally, atheism is present when the sense of meaning, personal dignity, basic trust, and individual vocation is in eclipse. When people cease to feel individually important, they turn to

Jehovah, God, and Allah as Idols
U.S.S.R.

some leader or state beyond themselves that claims to be the fulfillment of a divine destiny to try to fill the void. Lacking the still, small voice of personal conscience, or the call of personal destiny that can be heard only in solitude, the mass person submerges individuality and salutes the official "God" whose will is announced unambiguously in amplified form by radio, television, newspapers, and in torchlight parades.

God is dead when the only questions we ask are of expediency, power, and profit. When each individual, each nation, and the human species as a whole considers itself the aim, goal, sole purpose, for which life was created, then all other life becomes a means to narcissistic and nationalistic ends. When there are no restraints on our conduct, no moral limits beyond which we will not go to survive, no carnage, torture, or expenditure we will not sanction in the name of private advantage or national defense, then we are living godlessly, no matter how much we invoke the name of God.

The opposite of atheism—which I prefer to call "trust" rather than "faith," "wonder" rather than "belief," "living in the presence of the sacred" rather than "knowing God"—is rooted in the discipline of metanoia. We resist atheism only when we refuse to yield to the continual temptations to narcissism and nationalism, transcend the narrow limits of ego and group consciousness, and realize that the center is everywhere. The sacred is manifest in all places; God is a circle whose center is everywhere, whose circumference is nowhere. We are most human and nearest to what is holy when we move away from our well-guarded selves and move toward strangers and the encompassing mystery in which we live and move and have our being. The holy and human touch in that moment of self-transcendence that is the essence of freedom.

Enmity destroys freedom. Only lovers are free to come and go. Enemies dare not let each other out of sight. In the absence of being we cling to having; the vacuum of love is filled by hate.

Everything was peaceful in our valley until my neighbor to the north decided to install a locked gate across the road that provides the only access to the top part of my farm. Although a portion of the road does pass through his property, for more than fifty years the old road had been freely used by miners, homesteaders, ranchers, and hunters. But he insisted he had the right to exclusive use. Neither reason nor offer of compro-

Dollar Worship
U.S.S.R., 1950s

mise could dissuade him. Finally I cut the lock off the gate. He replaced it. I cut it off again. And again. Hostilities escalated when he placed his feedlot adjacent to the creek, polluting our drinking water. Once we nearly came to blows when we both happened to be near the disputed gate. I would have welcomed a good old-fashioned fist fight, but he has the advantage of money to squander on lawyers so he backed off. The matter drags on year after year. Every time I ride past the gate on my horse I get angry. On the days when I am wrestling with more demons than usual or bickering with my wife I go up and cut the damn lock off again and drive my truck on the road to assert my claim. Most recently, I hiked up the mountainside and rolled boulders on the road, blocking his way. In the process I strained myself so badly that I was in pain for nearly a month. But I had my revenge. Over the years I have become habituated to my enemy. He is never very far from mind. Whenever something unexpected happens—a fence broken, the creek muddied, a tool missing—my first thought is of him. I make him the scapegoat, the immediate explanation, the first cause of all my trouble, the snake in my garden. In my lucid moments I wonder whether I would be disappointed if he took the lock off the gate and started acting in a neighborly way.

The tyranny begins when we become fascinated by our enemy. In the beginning the insult, the offense, the intrusion is small. The wound is slight. We react to punish the aggressor, get even, reestablish order. He reacts to our reaction. The chain reaction of enmity begins.

Our focus narrows, our categories harden until we see the whole world through the lens of our struggle. All people are reduced to allies or foes. Every enemy of our enemy is a friend. Every friend must be an enemy of our enemy. The kaleidoscope of reality is reduced to a single either/or, for or against, black or white.

All energy is focused on the single life-or-death matter of defeating the enemy, destroying the evil one. Science is pressed into the service of creating new weapons. Everything on the home front is geared to help the war effort.

Our actions mirror what we imagine the enemy is going to do. We have no independent goals or foreign policy. Only a response to his malevolent intent. If we militarize our society it is only because we have discovered a bomber gap, tank gap, missile gap, megaton gap, spending gap. We have no initiative in the waging of peace. No department of peace. The enemy, after all, is intent upon world conquest, so we dare not let down our guard. And the choice of weapons and battlefields is his. If it were not for him, there would be peace in our valley.

Gradually we form ourselves in the image of what we hate. We become like the enemy. To defend free speech we impose censorship and limit the right of criticism of the military and government. We proclaim a state of emergency in which all vital information is "top secret." We draft our young men and force them to submit to the dehumanizing standardization of military discipline. The uniformity, loss of individuality, and servility the enemy wanted to impose upon us we adopt voluntarily "for the duration." However in the cold war of the last era the state of emergency has become permanent.

It becomes more and more difficult to imagine who we are without reference to our enemy. Our negative identity, or orientation *against* becomes primary. The enemy (COMMUNISM, CAPITALISM—always capitalized, larger than life) becomes our symbiotic partner. We become Siamese twins stabbing each other. In our infantile rage we fear the loss of the other. Without him who would we blame for the slings and arrows, the

Uncle Sam Crucifying Peace in Central America
Jose Luis Hernandes Espindola. Mexico

failures, the wounds, the inchoate anger, the gnawing frustration, the injustice? Better hatred than vertigo.

In the end the enemy becomes our explanation, motivation, and *raison d'être*. The images we have created become icons around which our existence is centered.

The mark of true atheism is not a theoretical disbelief in a being called "God" but the actual centering of one's existence around the enemy.

APPLIED DEMONOLOGY

Devils, Bureaucrats, and Fallen Angels

Propaganda is black magic.
The warlocks are in high places.
Not dancing in the glens.

Demon, Sixteenth-Century Style

Propaganda is an adult fairytale. Mirror, mirror on the wall, who is the fairest of them all? *Snow White*. And who the ugliest? *The Wicked Witch*. We are G(o)od. They are (D)evil. Now let's switch figure and ground. Claim the Devil as our own. Assume for a moment that he may symbolize some aspect of human experience we need to reclaim in order to be whole. The Devil, properly demythologized, may turn out to be one of the few enemies the United States and U.S.S.R. have in common.

The Devil, like the God of politics, is essentially created to allow us to deny responsibility for our actions. We pursue a manifest destiny because God demands it of us. And, if in the course of our sacred crusades to bring divine rule, the by-product is unspeakable suffering, this was caused by the enemy who is an agent of the Devil. So long as God and the Devil are rhetorically called up as explanations of war, we deny the moral reality and agency of both the self and the other. I (who have surrendered my will to the will of God) and You (who have surrendered your will to the Devil) are both relieved of personal responsibility for our actions. God made me do it. The Devil made the enemy do it.

In recent times the Devil has mostly worn a gray flannel suit and become a bureaucrat. Most evil in the modern world is done by anonymous men and women who serve the bureaucracies and mass armies without question. The willingness to obey the "authorities," to do what the boss tells us, not to question the orders of our superiors, to surrender private conscience to the goals of the group is a part of the job description. Evil has become a by-product of duty, an unfortunate consequence of loyalty. Nobody is really responsible when Ford produces Pintos that blow up on impact because

109

Demon, Twentieth-Century Style
Art Young, W.W. I

Evil rests on the passionate personal motive to perpetuate oneself.
Ernest Becker

of a faulty gas tank, or when artillery barrages "accidentally" fall on "friendly" villages. The sheer size of modern corporations, governments, and armies has made the application of techniques of mass production to people inevitable. Individuals are reduced to functions and must be, like parts of an efficient machine, interchangeable. To be is to fit in. In such bureaucracies, civilians are turned into soldiers, forced to wear uniforms, to submerge their autonomy and obey those above them in the hierarchy.

This submersion is equivalent to the abdication of the self as a moral agent, the surrender of control to a force outside ourselves. And to whatever we surrender we assign the prerogatives of God. It becomes the center, the *axis mundi*, the ultimate concern, the organizing principle of our lives. The idol becomes God. The Devil often masquerades in divine costume.

Both God and the Devil seem to testify to the abiding human experience of being possessed by alien forces, being out of control, being unable to achieve autonomy. And sometimes the power that sweeps us along is creative and other times destructive. Much as we struggle to control life, our illusion of omnipotence keeps breaking down and with it our feeling of safety. But if we cannot always stay in control, we can at least define that to which we must surrender as divine, so long as we can define the enemy's surrender to what cannot be controlled as demonic. Our schizophrenia, if not cured, can at least be baptized and controlled. I am not split between warring forces of good and evil. Propaganda allows us to exteriorize the battle, project the struggle within the psyche into the realm of politics.

The Devil will never lose his power until we claim him as our own, acknowledging that he is a symbol for a deep and universal human experience. Medieval theology recognized this truth when it pictured Satan as a fallen angel whose home was originally with God. The psychological insight encapsulated in the symbol of the Devil is that we are often enslaved by goodness gone mad. The evil we experience and do, springs from virtue gone rancid, unbalanced vitality. Our will to live, to create, to serve the cause of the good, to progress, to form communities, carries with it inevitable tragic consequences. We excel only by reducing others to the status of inferiors; win only by creating a majority of losers. One man's triumph is another's defeat.

Every historical age has a different experience of what it is that is out of control, and thus a different content to its demonology. When credal orthodoxy and unwavering belief in religious dogma was a social requirement for salvation, the Devil became the doubter, the blasphemer, the disbeliever. Once Descartes proclaimed doubt a virtue (*Dubito ergo sum*) and the age of reason was born, the Devil became the incarnation of irrationality. Consistently he has borne the burden of our embarrassment about the body—he dwells in filth, excrement, sexuality, especially in men's repressed fears and resentments toward women. He is the archseducer whose worship involves black masses and sexual orgies. He works through witches, wanton women, and temptresses—whose vaginas were declared the devil's gate by more than one church father. In our time the Devil is not so much the doubter and sexual seducer as the symbol of the hubris of an insane technology. He is Mephistopheles, Faust, the mad scientist Frankenstein, the incarnation of perverse creativity.

When we describe the Devil thus as the organized or systematic obsession with power that has been divorced from purpose, the mindless will-to-power, it is clear that this ancient symbol is profoundly relevant to modern experience. Bureaucracies and the contemporary state have functioned in a satanic manner to allow us to commit the most hideous crimes and to deny responsibility for them. The German extermination camps and the systematic slaughter of civilian populations in Russia, Cambodia, Indonesia, China, Pakistan, and so on, *ad nauseum*, have been carried out by men who have all been "following orders," "doing their duty." The state "made them do it" in the same way that the Devil ordered the "Son of Sam" to commit murders in New York.

At the present moment, both the United States and the U.S.S.R. feel themselves to be possessed by the modern equivalent of the Devil—the creative-demonic power of runaway technology that threatens to end the world with a whimper or a bang, ecological pollution or nuclear warfare. If the acid rain, the greenhouse effect, the erosion of our soil, the destruction of our air and watersheds do not destroy us, the nuclear winter may. Technology in general, and weapons technology in particular, seems to have developed its own momentum. It is a demon out of control, pushing us to create new generations of computers and weapons systems with dizzying speed. Both countries feel themselves powerless to refrain from building yet more suicidal weapons. Both operate as if there were implicit within

Runaway
Robert Bastian. San Francisco Chronicle
1966

The Adversary
Oliphant, by Pat Oliphant. Copyright, 1983,
Universal Press Sindicate. Used by permission.
All rights reserved.

The Soviet Union and the United States face an impersonal adversary that overrides any specific threat one side may see in the other. The adversary is the looming danger of nuclear war.

Georgi Arbatov, Director, Moscow Institute for American and Canadian Studies

technology an imperative that demands that what can be made *must* be made. And if we do not produce the ultimate weapons, our enemies will. The theme is commonly expressed in the science fiction scenarios of the machines rebelling and taking over the world. In international affairs, we have the specter of communities of scientists continuing to invent weapons that nobody wants because they feel that they have no alternative. The angelic power of technology has been distorted into the satanic impulse to accumulate power that has no purpose other than destruction. Whether we are willing to use the ancient symbol or not, it is clear that we are in the grip of the experience of disowned responsibility, feigned impotence, and blind lust for power that traditionally was described as being possessed by the Devil.

The immense hope that might arise from the recognition of our disowned power to create evil (or good) lies in our making common cause against a common enemy. Nothing has the power to unite former enemies as quickly as the emergence of a common enemy. *Russia and America are currently being captured by the same Devil and hence are potential allies.*

In international as well as in interpersonal relations, re-owning our projections, giving up our illusions of impotence and innocence can lead us into responsible, purposeful, and satisfying modes of action. Every path to peace requires us to reclaim the Devil as our own and accept limits to our power. Either the United States

112

THE ENEMY AS BEAST, REPTILE, INSECT

1

2

3

4

1. U.S.S.R. **2.** Australia, W.W.I **3.** On helmet: Junta. Uncle Sam: "El Salvador marches on the path of peace and democracy"—U.S.S.R. **4.** I.R.A., Ireland

1. Hitler as Rat. "We will defeat and destroy our enemy without mercy." On paper: The non-aggression pact between U.S.S.R. and Germany—U.S.S.R., W.W.II
2. U.S.S.R. as Octopus
3. Netherlands, W.W.II
4. Italy, W.W.II **5.** Nazi party as threatening snake—Germany **6.** U.S. as spider creeping over Spain—U.S.S.R.

1

2

3

4

1. The Bolshevik Chameleon — Germany, W.W.II
2. Enemies of the Revolution as chicken-footed reptiles — Nicaragua **3.** "Leave us alone, Jews. De Gaulle Lies."— Occupied France, W.W.II **4.** U.S., W.W.II

1. Nixon as Vampire—
Southeast Asia **2.** America
as Paper Tiger—China
3. "Defeat the Maurading
Fascists."—U.S.S.R., W.W.II
4. A rare instance in which a
modern nation identifies its
heroic warrior with an
animal—Italy, W.W.II

HEROIC WARFARE: THE ENEMY AS WORTHY OPPONENT

In the authentic tradition of heroic warfare the warrior knew the name, the character, and the history of his enemy and granted him the respect due a fellow warrior.

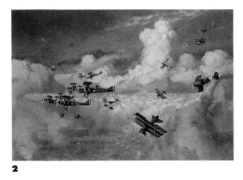

1. 13th Century. When knighthood was in flower.
2. Fighter pilots such as the Red Baron and Eddie Ricken-backer became legendary for duels in the air—W.W.I (George Horace Davis)
3. Samurai warriors in ceremonial combat **4.** German duelists. The heroic ideal was kept alive in the 20th century by professional military elites.

Modern propagandists have made use of the iconography of heroic warfare in a degraded way, combining an inflated self-portrait of the hero with a degraded portrayal of the enemy.

1

2

3

4

5

Modern Knights?

1. Hitler the Heroic Leader—Germany, W.W.II
2. Portrait of Japanese as Samurai—Italy, W.W.II
3. "Those who come to us with the sword will perish by the sword." The modern warrior is linked to the ancient hero—U.S.S.R., W.W.II

And Revolutionary Heroes.

4. The Spirit of 76. Are revolutionaries still heroes?
5. "Long live Chairman Mao's cultural revolution." In theory, in Marxism the people are the hero. In fact, the cult of personality is still central—China **6.** "Sandino Lives." The modern individual soldier reenacts the myth, partakes of the story, the name, and the courage of the original hero. In mass armies symbolic identification replaces individual combat—Nicaragua
7. Heroic triumph over the technological monster—Vietnam

Sandino vive en la Lucha por la Paz !

6

7

THE ENEMY AS ABSTRACTION

Modern warfare increasingly erases the face, the name, and the individuality of both the warrior and the enemy. The human image gradually disappears and is replaced by portraits of weapons.

3

1

2

4

5

1. The machine gun, the submarine, and the airplane changed the nature of war, made it anonymous. Civilians now lived on the battleground and had to be able to identify the enemy—Britain, W.W.I
2. Image used by U.S. army to teach soldiers to identify the enemy. Note the blank face—U.S., W.W.II **3.** A bird's-eye view. In aerial warfare the enemy becomes an abstraction seen from a great distance—Italy, W.W.II **4.** May Day Soviet Style. Modern warfare is less a fight between people or nations than an ideological battle between "communist" and "capitalist" empires connected to opposite ends of a trip-wire that may detonate the nuclear doomsday.
5. Europe United against Bolshevism. Faceless enemies—France, W.W.II

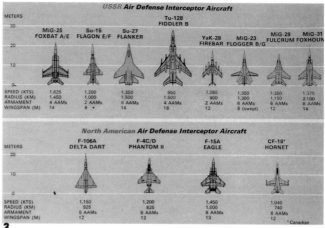

1. Advertisement, 1984
2. The human image, either of the warrior or the enemy, appears less and less frequently in modern portrayals of war. The weapons themselves are the new icons of *Homo hostilis*. In the old style, the enemy was portrayed larger than life to motivate us to fight. In the new style of ideological paranoia, the weapons of the enemy are portrayed as more threatening than ours. We perceive a "weapons gap" that justifies our increase in armaments. The enemy has the same perception—U.S. Defense Dept., 1985 **3.** The world according to them **4.** An early version of "Star Wars," the technological hope for a machine to end war—France, 1890–1910

and the U.S.S.R. will continue to worship the same Devil and will conspire unconsciously to create a nuclear Armageddon, or we will recognize that we have a common adversary and will embrace each other as allies.

THE BARBARIAN ON THE BORDER

The Uncivilized Libido

The AntiCommunist as Barbarian
U.S.S.R.

Civilization is a constant struggle to hold back the forces of barbarism. With great sacrifice and discipline, the ego establishes a tenuous rule of law and order and makes a clearing in the jungle. But at any moment, the undomesticated powers threaten to disrupt us because, in truth, we are terribly ambivalent about the achievements of civilization.

As Freud observed, civilization is always accompanied by discontent. Something in us still wants to run wild, follow every impulse to its satiation, lose ourselves in an orgy of sex and violence and indolence. Look carefully and you will see the hairy legs of the satyr protruding from the Hickey-Freedman suit. We fear and long for our wildness to emerge.

The barbarian, the giant running amok, the uncivilized enemy, symbolize power divorced from intelligence, animal cunning without the gentling hand of spirit. It is what Plato thought of as unformed or chaotic matter, and Freud called the libido, an amoral psychic force. Just as "civilized" nations have always justified their exploitation of raw resources of "backward" countries because it was their duty to bring them into the forward march of reason and progress, so the ego has harnessed the barbarous energy of the libido. The warrior who defeats the barbarian, like the hero who descends into the depths of the psyche and returns with the boon of consciousness, is a servant of mind, intelligence, spirit—a culture hero.

The image of the enemy as barbarian has been an integral part of the formation of the psychological and political identity of most "advanced" societies. The barbarian forms a kind of psychological bottom line that defines how far "civilized" people are allowed to descend. So long as "they" are defined as dumb and cruel, "we" are saved from having to look at our own stupidity and sadism. As modern people have increasingly viewed themselves as reasonable and nice, they have had to find some target on which to project their denied

The Pentagon—Mindless Power
U.S.S.R.

will-to-power, their savagery, their blood lust, their rampant sexuality.

Periodically the Apollonian mask of society shatters and we plunge into a perverted form of the Dionysian orgy—warfare—which provides us an occasion to unleash our barbarism. In battle all men are free to give vent to their hatred, frustration, and lust for destruction.

Generation after generation, we kill the barbarian. So long as we refuse to re-own the shadow of our own savagery projected onto the enemy, warfare remains a blind ritual where "ignorant armies clash by night," a repetition compulsion, an addiction. Without consciousness, there is no catharsis. Without catharsis, no novelty. Without novelty, no future that transcends our barbarous past.

THE INSATIABLE PSYCHE

Concupiscence and Conquest

Capitalists Profiting from Vietnam War
U.S.S.R.

Contentment is probably the rarest of all human virtues. No matter how much we have, few of us are satisfied. We always want more. We seem to be the frustrated species.

There are many explanations for our insatiability. Marx attributed it to the injustice and exploitation that resulted from the conflict between capitalists and workers. Freud discovered the libido as the source of the discontent that accompanies civilization. Modern capitalism assumes happiness is an automatic result of owning designer jeans or the latest-model automobile. Medieval theologians called the endless desire "concupiscence" and saw it as the cause of Lucifer's fall from heaven and the human fall from grace.

Concupiscence takes many forms in modern life. In industrial countries, it is the lust for consumer goods. Both the credit card revolution and the sexual revolution were based on the assumption that all desires should be satisfied instantly. Economically, concupiscence comes disguised as the technological dogma of inexhaustible resources and the possibility of an ever-escalating gross national product. Politically it is manifest as the drive for power and empire. All forms share

Consuming Passion
Aislin. The Gazette. Montreal
© 1985 by Cartoonists and Writers Syndicate

Will he stuff it?
Aportes. Sandinista publication

Since 1945, few nations have been willing to argue openly for political imperialism. Instead international power is interpreted ideologically and justified as a responsibility to advance peaceful world revolution or to protect freedom and liberty against totalitarianism.
Sue Mansfield

the assumption that there are no limits to human desires or capacities, no possibility of having enough.

Clearly, the disease of concupiscence is universal. A simple look at a world map will confirm that the propaganda charges of both the United States and the U.S.S.R. are accurate. Along with China, we are the great modern insatiables. We have lost any sense of our natural borders or legitimate spheres of influence. The three great world empires are each omnivorous, devouring everything in their paths, extending their control by trade and/or conquest. And all deny that they are imperialists. Recently, when I presented a slide lecture on "Faces of the Enemy" in the Soviet Union, I concluded my presentation by saying, "I have just returned from Nicaragua and have been profoundly disturbed by what I saw there. My country is bullying a small and poor nation that has an imperfect government but nevertheless the best it has had in 100 years. With our appetite for empire, I would hate to be a neighbor of the United States." My audience smiled and nodded approval. Then I continued, "When I read about what is happening in Poland and Afghanistan and see your appetite for empire, I also would not want to be a neighbor of the Soviet Union." Knowing looks darted over some faces as a chorus of objection was whispered: "Afghanistan is not like Vietnam. Poland is not like Nicaragua." In fairness, I must admit that I have received the same reaction in Washington, D.C. All nations claim to be modest and moderate in their needs. "We are not lusting after empire." Like the Texas rancher, all we want is the land that is rightfully ours and what borders on it. We are both insatiable and embarrassed by our inability to be content with our common wealth.

St. Augustine suggested that the only cure for concupiscence was to discover what desires were satiable and what were not. "Thou hast made us for Thyself and our hearts are restless till they rest in Thee," he said. Human beings have a destiny that transcends the moment, therefore we are rightfully restless. We are *Homo viator*, pilgrims, an incomplete species. The promise that sleeps in our genes is not yet fulfilled. The intentionality that is programmed into our DNA has not yet achieved its natural goal, its *telos*. The genetic information we carry is never wholly inscribed on the pages of our days. Insofar as we honor the vocation that calls us toward a Beyond we can never fully comprehend or adequately symbolize, toward a human future that is prefigured only in our highest present

Remember. We are here to defend the security of the United States.

Roger. Barricada. Nicaragua
© 1985 by Cartoonists and Writers Syndicate

moments, we will always be animated by an urgency toward something beyond our reach. This nostalgia for completeness, far from being satiable by consuming or conquest, is the token of the human capacity for transcendence. If we allow the metaphysical hunger to remain without trying to satiate it with substitutes—we find it is the sacred void, the *ex nihilo*, from which creativity arises.

Paradoxically, it is accepting the unlimited reaches of the human spirit that allows us to be content within the limits of what is presently possible. Mortal pleasures are sufficient for mortal satisfaction when more is not asked of them. The enlightened person, according to Zen Buddhism, has learned the true miracle of human consciousness—to be satisfied with what is given. The master of everyday life eats when he eats and sleeps when he sleeps and is content.

To move beyond the warrior psyche, we must create a sustainable psyche, we must recognize and rejoice within the limits of growth. Both ecologically and psychologically the new heroic images we need are of men and women who can aspire to create psychic and political possibilities that now seem utopian and at the same time be satisfied with the moment.

THE SADOMASOCHISM OF EVERYDAY LIFE

The Need for Vindictive Triumph

We force the enemy to wear the mask of the sadist to preserve the best-kept secret of civilized life: humankind is not kind. We take a perverse pleasure in visiting cruelty and death on our fellows. So long as we do not have to admit that sadism is present in the majority, we do not have to make a serious study of what produces the appetite for cruelty, killing, and vengeance in some and accounts for the equally strong repugnance to kill or torture in others.

Sadism in war is hard to explain only if we assume that there is a discontinuity between soldiers who enjoy inflicting pain and normal men and women. The assumption that there is a vast difference between the moral fiber of the man who enjoys killing in battle and you and me is the illusion on which the notion of normality is built. Normal people, we like to believe, are nice, moderate, and mannerly. Not unduly angry or

Right-wing students in Thailand massacre a left-wing student. Note the pleasure of the spectators.
© 1976 by Neal Uleviche, Wide World

I enjoyed the shooting and the killing. I was literally turned on when I saw a gook get shot. When a GI got shot, even if I didn't know him . . . that would bother me. A GI was real. But if a gook got killed, it was like me going out here and stepping on a roach.
Mark Baker

cruel. Civilized people are supposedly civil, law abiding, respectful of the rights of others. They do not abuse their children or inflict unnecessary pain on others.

Let's switch perspectives for a moment and try on the hypothesis that society is an intricate sadomasochistic system.

The essence of sadomasochism is the interplay between two persons, one of whom is defined as top and the other as bottom. The top, dominant or sadist, overtly controls and humiliates the bottom, passive or masochist. Pain is the coin that measures the exchange of power. The sadist inflicts pain to demonstrate that he

> *The history of childhood is a nightmare from which we have only recently begun to awaken. The further back in history one goes, the lower the level of child care, and the more likely children are to be killed, abandoned, beaten, terrorized, and sexually abused.*
>
> Lloyd DeMause

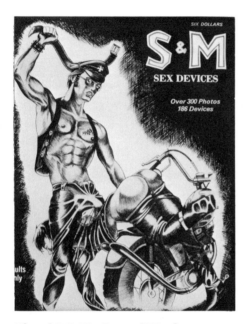

Ritual S & M. Sexual Warfare

or she is in command. The masochist submits to pain to demonstrate that he or she is willing to be submissive. When sadomasochism reaches the level of a conscious sexual ritual where the roles are acted out, there is always an agreement about how far the humiliation and punishment are to go. In fact, in most formalized sadomasochist relationships, it is the masochist who sets the limits and is in charge of the ritual. In unconscious, and therefore most compulsive sadomasochistic exchanges, the sadist may seize, torture, and kill a person who is truly innocent. For every situation in which the sadomasochistic violence is in some way agreed on by both parties, there are hundreds of cases where rampant sadism is visited on innocent victims. Rape is very occasionally a perverse transaction between perpetrator and "victim." It is usually an act of unsolicited sadism.

If we take the defining characteristic of sadomasochism—an exchange of power between a dominant and a submissive in which some degree of humiliation and pain is visited on the "bottom" by the "top"—we can see that society is arranged hierarchically to allow such exchanges to take place in a ritualized and "normal" way. Traditionally men have been tops, women, slaves, and ethnic minorities the bottoms. All but the most egalitarian tribes have social hierarchies that allow people in one rank to submit to those above them and dominate those below. We like to believe this enormous dominance-submission system was both natural and relatively kindly. But it is hard to maintain this illusion if we look at the historical evidence. Masters owned and used slaves as they pleased. Until the advent of unions, employers required their powerless employees to work in inhumane conditions. The good bourgeois of England had no compunction about forcing children of eight and nine years to work twelve hours in mines. A look at the history of childhood will show that what we now consider child abuse was the ordinary practice in most premodern societies.

Even in recent times children have been cruelly treated under the guise of "discipline." It is not difficult to see the roots of the Nazi sadism in the normal methods of German child rearing. I recently did seminars in Germany and found that almost every one in my groups had been physically beaten as a child. As Alice Miller shows in *For Your Own Good*, normal and even "good" parents routinely inflict much abuse and inadvertent suffering on their children. It still pains my mother to tell how under doctors' orders she allowed me to cry until the appointed time for my four-hour feeding had arrived, lest she spoil me. Those of biblical faith have for generations lived by the motto: Spare the rod and spoil the child. It is only recently that a non-sadistic mode of child rearing has emerged as an idea.

The history of our wounds is largely repressed. Since our early pain is inflicted on us by those on whom we depended for survival and love, we cannot be openly rageful without risking punishment or abandonment. Thus we "forget" the pain and put aside our ambivalent love-hate for the parents who nurtured and wounded us and bury our need for revenge under masks of politeness and manners. The middle class is the conspiracy of moderation designed to cover up the wild love and fierce hatred that is the legacy of childhood. It creates a façade that hides what Arthur Janov called the "primal pool of pain," a personality that allows us to continue to play the up-down games of parent-child in socially acceptable ways. The exchange of power between superior and inferior is predicated on an unconscious need of one to become the vengeful parent and of the other to become the obedient child, who by submitting, may finally win the love of the phantom parent.

In the degree that we have been wounded, we will be wounding. Abused children become abusing parents—unless they remain conscious of the cruelty they suffered and make an effort to love their children as they wished to be loved when they were children.

Our unconscious wounds produce cruelty in varying degrees and manners. The need for "vindictive triumph" (the essence of neurosis or "normal" sadomasochism) takes many forms. Some people turn the cruelty inward and become self-hating, torturing themselves with constant feelings of guilt, a tyranny of the "shoulds," a harsh and scrupulous conscience. Others will punish themselves with continual failure or disease. Still others will turn their hatred outward and become heartless employers or power-obsessed entrepreneurs. Wherever individuals or nations become obsessed with power (rather than pleasure or compassion), the driving force is unconscious sadism.

In warfare our cruelty is allowed a periodic catharsis. We visit on symbolic objects the frustration and rage we have accumulated from all the wounds and humiliations we have suffered. How strange, haunting, even touching our cruelty is. When we look closely, we find that hatred is a form of tortured love. Generation after generation, we go to war to vindicate our parents.

FDR as Assassin of Civilians
France, W.W. II

The enemy was cruel, it was clear, yet this did not trouble me as deeply as did our own cruelty. Indeed, their brutality made fighting the Germans much easier, whereas ours weakened the will and confused the intellect.
Glenn Gray

U.S. as Oppressor
U.S.S.R.

The Terrorist Olympics: U.S. in Second Place
Gomma Farhat
© 1985 by Cartoonists and Writers Syndicate

Never daring to feel the horror of being wounded by those we most love, never daring to accuse them of cruelty, we find surrogates on whom we can dump the burden of our rage. Rather than weeping for our woundedness and daring to express our hurt and anger and risk the final abandonment, we recreate shadow dramas to purge the violence that seethes beneath our moderate and mannerly personalities.

To lessen the quantity of cruelty and sadism, we must learn to listen to the cry beneath violence. The victor must hear himself in the victim's cry, the winner feel himself in the humiliation of the loser. It is always the sad, the wounded, the disappointed child in ourselves we seek to triumph over, to deny, in defeating the enemy. So long as we can visit pain on another, we need not feel our own pain. Anger lifts depression. For a time, purging our rage on a scapegoat relieves us of the feeling. But the need for the cleansing of the unacceptable feelings builds up, and we must plunge into a new circle of violence. The only certain way out of the blind ritual of war is by learning to substitute grief for anger. Those who mourn the childhood love they never had, who treat their own wounds tenderly, learn to forgive and to break the vicious circle of the wounded and the wounding. Every day we are not grieving is a day we will be taking vengeance. When we are unable to confess that our own parents, our own governments, our own styles of life, have disappointed and injured us, we will inevitably create an enemy on whom we heap our anger. The Soviets must find a scapegoat on whom to lay the burden of pain caused by World War II, the purges of Stalin, and the continuing brutality of their own bureaucracy. The United States must find a scapegoat on whom to lay the pain of the disappointment in the American dream and the increasing frustration of life in a high-tech, low-touch society. Thus we form a blood bond, a community of enmity, where we agree to play a game of sadomasochistic politics. In the race to prevail, to be superior, to play the part of the sadist, each nation inflicts increasing economic hardship and political tyranny on its own people. The old, the young, the ill, must suffer deprivation so we can triumph over our enemies. The sadomasochistic drama of everyday life is complete when we define "normal" relations as a process of perpetual planning and national sacrifice directed at achieving the means to destroy the other. The militarization of society *is* the triumph of sadomasochism.

RAPACIOUS NORMALITY

The War Between the Sexes

American Soldier as Seducer
Germany, W.W.II

A lady in doubt. Everything you do serves the victor. What does "everything" mean?
Germany, W.W.II

Rape is a necessary part of the ritual of warfare. Whether it happens seldom or often, no war is symbolically won until the enemy is humiliated by the abuse of "his" women. Psychologically speaking, the sexual territory of the enemy must be occupied and possessed. Men will understand neither themselves nor the nature of warfare until the psychological dynamics of *Homo hostilis* are seen clearly.

Let me begin with some statements that may at first seem preposterous. In large measure, war is a form of sexual perversion. The continuing battle between the sexes is abnormal even if practiced by a majority. The violence we regularly visit on the enemy is related to the systematic violence we have first committed on ourselves. The neglected truth, and therefore neglected hope, in a psychological rather than purely political understanding of war will emerge only if we look long and hard at some obvious but ignored elements of the war system.

First. War is a man's game. With very few exceptions, women have never organized or taken part in systematic violence. They have so seldom been warriors that without fear of rebuke we can use the masculine pronoun in discussing the history of war. Women have traditionally been pictured as supporting and nurturing their warriors, and they have entered into the romance of war by considering a man in uniform as especially masculine and desirable. But to the best of our knowledge there have been no matriarchical societies in which women organized mass violence against other societies.

Second. For roughly the last 10,000 to 13,000 years, the male has been socialized and informed primarily by the imperative to become a warrior. During this time we have cultivated reason, inquiry, artistic sensibilities, political skills, technological abilities, and many other capacities. But all the while, in the majority of societies, the male has been conditioned to be willing to kill or to die to defend the tribe or nation against its enemies. The single greatest difference between men and women, other than the obvious biological differences, is that the male must win the title of "man" by becoming a potential killer, while women retain the luxury of innocence. Almost universally the rites of passage for the male involve some painful ordeal—beatings, hazing, circumcision, fasting, killing an enemy or wild animal—in which the elders teach the young that men

War is a disease caused by an excess of testosterone.

It's a man's world

The New Leda
Germany, W.W.II

must be able to suffer in silence, fight, and be brave. Battle itself is seen as the baptism of fire, a wound as "the red badge of courage." Any man who fails to acquire the martial virtues is considered less than masculine. Phillip Caputo, speaking of the first "fire-fight" his platoon had in Vietnam, says,

> As I moved from one man to the next, I became aware of a subtle difference among them, and I might not have noticed it if I had not known them so intimately. They had taken part in their first action, though a minor one that had lasted only ninety minutes. But their company had killed during those ninety minutes; they had seen violent death for the first time and something of the cruelty combat arouses in men. Before the fire-fight, those marines fit both definitions of the word *infantry*, which means either a "body of soldiers equipped for service on foot," or "infants, boys, youths collectively." The difference was that the second definition could no longer be applied to them. Having received that primary sacrament of war, baptism of fire, their boyhoods were behind them. Neither they nor I thought of it in those terms at the time. We didn't say to ourselves, we've been under fire, we've shed blood, now we're men. We were simply aware, in a way we could not express, that something significant had happened to us.[28]

Third. The warrior psyche is created by a systematic destruction in the male of all "feminine" characteristics. In order to be a good warrior, a man must learn not to cry, not to yield to the body's demand for comfort and sensual enjoyment. To fight we must gird up our loins, toughen ourselves, feel no pain, no fear, disregard the will to live, and sacrifice life for the higher good of the tribe. Drill instructors in the Marines are following an ancient military tradition when they insult recruits by calling them "sissies," "pussies," or "cunts," in order to try to get them to become good soldiers. Some African tribes surgically remove men's nipples to exorcise all traces of femininity from those who were destined to become warriors. And Gilbert Herdt notes,

> The Sambia of New Guinea are typical of warrior societies in their suspicions and repression of the feminine: "A society of warriors tends to regard women as unkindly, and Sambia attitudes have carried this emphasis to its furthest recess. . . . The rhetoric and ritual of men represents women as

The Warrior must first conquer his own femininity
Jeanette Stobie

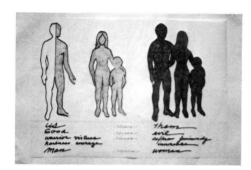

The Warrior Psyche and the Battle between the Sexes
Jeanette Stobie

Fear has made of women—as it has of peoples of color and Jews—symbols of feeling, carnality, nature, all that is in civilization's unconscious and that it would deny.
Susan Griffin

polluting inferiors a man should distrust throughout his life. Men hold themselves to be the superiors of women in physique, personality, and social position. Indeed, survival for individual and community alike demands hard, disciplined men as unlike the softness of women as possible. It forms the bedrock on which are based warfare, economics, production, and religious life. . . . Men idiomatically refer to women as a distinctively inferior and "darker" species than themselves.[29]

In the patriarchal tradition, which has created the warrior psyche, both the female and the feminine virtues have been degraded. Women and all things feminine must be kept in control. As Nietzsche said, "When you go to a woman do not forget the whip."

Fourth. The sexuality of the warrior is a blend of repressed homosexuality and phallic assertion. A boy is made into a warrior by removing him (usually between the ages nine and twelve) from the influence of women and placing his care and training in the hands of men. Among the Sambia, explicit homosexual rituals are involved. An initiate can become a warrior only by years of ritual fellatio, swallowing the seed of older warriors. Although most groups do not make the homosexual elements of war so obvious, it is just as present. To become a soldier, a man must submit to a superior officer, sacrifice his individuality, be broken in some equivalent of boot camp, identify with the history of military heroes. Within the context of battle, men grow to love each other and often sacrifice themselves to their love. Seemingly, it is only the matrix of violence that allows the emergence of tenderness in the warrior psyche. John Wayne can cradle a dying man in his arms, even shed a fugitive tear, but cannot touch another man in tenderness without raising the specter of being "queer." So threatening is any overt homosexuality, that in 1984 the U.S. military discharged 1,796 homosexuals on whom they had spent $22.5 million to recruit and train. One of the ways in which the warrior covers up his unconscious hostility toward the feminine and his latent homosexuality is by phallic aggression. His penis, instead of being a potential means of expressing tenderness, becomes a tool, a rod, a gun. To have sex with a woman is to "bang" her. Gang rape becomes a "gang-bang," a ritual of latent homosexual warriors who prove to themselves that they are "real" men by degrading a woman.

131

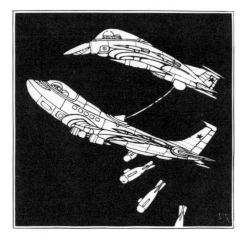

Erotic perversion
EMK. Aftonbladet. Stockholm Sweden. ©
1985 by Cartoonists and Writers Syndicate.

Homo hostilis can never be at peace because both the traditional warrior's psyche and the woman's psyche, artificially informed by the myth of war, are socially constructed in such a way as to make intrapsychic conflict and conflict between the sexes inevitable. When society molds men into warriors, it creates a systematic antagonism between the conscious egoideal and the unconscious or repressed potentialities of both men and women and artificially polarizes the sexes.

The psychological structure of the traditional warrior and the women that have thus far been created by the habit of warfare may be summarized as follows:

In the degree that women have recently entered into the public world of business and government and have begun to define themselves as competitors and executives, they have started to take on many of the personality characteristics (and diseases of stress) of the warrior.

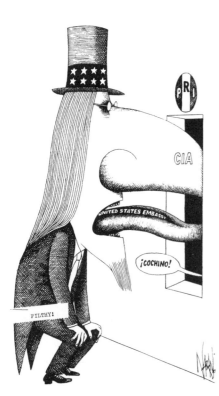

Filthy
Rogelio Naranjo. El Universal. Mexico
© 1985 by Cartoonists and Writers Syndicate

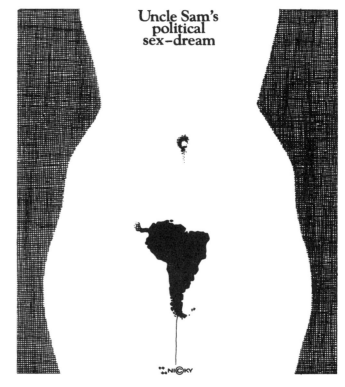

America's Sex Dream
Nicolas Pecareff. Bulgaria
© 1985 by Cartoonists and Writers Syndicate

The Warrior

Ego ideal Consciously:	*Shadow* Unconsicously:
He is expected to protect, to suffer, to kill, and to die. His body and character are hardened to allow him to fight.	He is fragile and terrified of his tenderness and mortality.
His psyche centers in reason, will. He is spirit, mind.	Moody, lacking skill in dealing with emotion.
He is dominant, cruel, sadistic.	Covertly submissive and passive.
His defining virtue is power.	His controlling fear is impotence.
He strives for independence, self-definition.	He is unconsciously controlled by dependency needs, surrenders to and obeys authority.
He is allowed anger but no tears.	Grief and melancholy cause his depression.
He is supposed to be brave, bold, aggressive.	He represses his fear and shyness.
His sphere of action is public, political.	He has abandoned the familiar and domestic.
He is extroverted, practical, focused, linear, goal oriented; at worst, obsessive and rigid.	He fears feeling, nature, woman, death, all that evades his efforts to control.
As actor he assumes super responsibility and Promethean guilt.	Arrogance and pride shadow his life.

The Woman

Ego idea Consciously:	*Shadow* Unconsciously:
She is expected to inspire, to nurture, to heal. Her body and character are softened to allow her to care.	She is tough and terrified of her power.
Her psyche centers in emotion and sensation. She is nature, body.	Opinionated, lacking skill in disciplined thinking.
She is submissive, obedient, masochistic.	Covertly manipulative and cruel.
Her defining virtue is warmth.	Her controlling fear is frigidity.
She strives for relationship, belonging.	She is unconsciously controlled by rebellious emotions and fears of self-definition and freedom.
She is allowed tears but no anger.	Resentment and rage cause her depression.
She is supposed to be fearful, shy, passive.	She represses her boldness and agression.
Her sphere of action is private, domestic.	She has abandoned the worldly and political.
She is introverted, intuitive, unfocused, cyclical, process oriented; at worst, hysterical and atonic.	She fears abstraction, history, man, power politics, all that evades the logic of her heart.
As reactor she becomes victim, blamer, martyr.	Timidity and low self-esteem shadow her life.

But to date, they have remained innocent of the single most important defining activity of the warrior—the systematic education in violence and the willingness to kill. Short of entering fully into the power-violence-killing game women will not gain equal political and economic power with men and the traditional psychological structures will remain.

The conclusion seems inevitable. Once men have destroyed their own "femininity" in order to mold themselves into warriors, they will inevitably perceive women as a subspecies of the enemy, a threat to their integrity, and will live with civil war within the self, the war between the sexes, and political war between nations. Those who live by the sword perceive all reality, inner and outer, through the metaphor of war.

Recorded human history roughly coincides with the era of *Homo hostilis*. From this we may conclude that human beings are innately hostile, territorial animals. Or we may, after studying the intricate social process necessary to create and sustain the warrior psyche, conclude that we do not yet know very much about the human psyche. What would the male psyche be like if it was not systematically desensitized, subjected to a taboo on tenderness? What would the female psyche be like if it was not forbidden overt aggression? What kind of psyche would we create by raising children in an atmosphere in which the warfare between the sexes was absent? If we ceased to consider the rapacious psyche normal, a new type of man and woman might emerge and for the first time we might know what we were when we were not separated by gender-related, psychic, and political conflict.

THE HUMAN BEAST

On the Warfare Against Nature

That we regularly use a whole repertoire of animal, reptile, and insect images to dehumanize our enemies shows us the extent to which modern technological societies are rooted in a metaphysic of war against nature. Once upon a time, snake, bear, dog, lion, wolf, were all considered totem animals, sacred spirits, familial powers. Men and women took animal names, belonged to clans named in honor of wild things, admired the cunning of Coyote, the industry of Ant, the grace of Hawk, the resurrecting spirit of Snake. Beasts were family, not enemies. Modernity began when we began to conceive of nature as a state of perpetual warfare, "red in tooth and claw," a struggle in which only the fittest survive. And in the state of nature, man was a raving wolf who could be civilized only by a social contract. We learned to congratulate ourselves with titles designed to show that we could transcend nature. We were not Bearman or Snakewoman, but *Homo sapiens*, *Homo faber*. Our reason and our ability to make tools set us above the animals, gave us the right to dominate. Science, conceived of as a mode of torture—"putting nature on the rack" and forcing her to answer our ques-

134

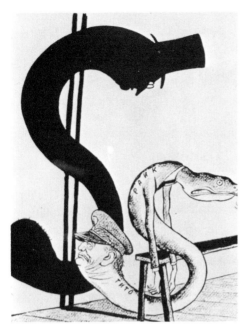

Truman and Tito as Snake
U.S.S.R.

tions—gave us the means to become supernatural, to become lords over matter.

In so far as our claim to dignity is rooted in our ability to transcend nature, it becomes necessary to find a way to deny our animality. We bathe to remove smell, dress to cover the body, create cities in which we are hermetically sealed against any intrusion of weather. Then we place animals in controlled environments— zoos—where we can watch them from a safe distance. All the while we destroy natural environments, using resources to turn matter into cultural artifacts.

If the enemy can be relegated to the domain of nature, it follows from the logic of our supernatural metaphysic, that he is a means, an *it*, a bit of raw material with which we are morally entitled to do anything we desire. Indeed, as the bearers of reason we have a moral obligation to tame the bestial powers and put matter to good use.

The two major problems that will have to be solved if we are to survive long beyond the twentieth century— the habit of warfare and ecological pollution—are two

The Paper Tiger of U.S. Technology Defeated
Vietnam

Dean Acheson as Dog
U.S.S.R.

Tid for ømhet?

**Reagan with Sven Straz,
Minister of Foreign Affairs, on his back**
Hallvard Skauge. Norway
© 1985 by Cartoonists and Writers Syndicate

sides of a single coin. When we define ourselves as superior to our neighbors and to nature, we inevitably create a hostile environment, an ecology of violence. Advertising, which encourages us to turn the natural world into things, and propaganda, which invites us to turn our neighbors into things, are both instruments of a metaphysic of total warfare, a paranoid vision in which we are surrounded by an alien world. The solution to both problems lies in the same vein—the development of a psyche and a polis organized around being *with* rather than being *against*. The task that faces us is nothing less than rethinking and recreating ourselves, our view of nature, our institutions. It is hard to imagine how we can change from a psychology, metaphysic, and politic of alienation to one of kindness. It is harder yet to imagine that we will survive if we cannot get beyond hostility to kinship.

THERE IS ONLY ONE KIND OF PRESSURE...

USA

Nicaragua
Roger. Barricada, Nicaragua
© 1985 by Cartoonists and Writers Syndicate

DEATH

The Final Enemy

War is a means of maximizing death in the guise of minimizing death, of creating surplus evil in the guise of destroying evil. The paradox can be understood only from within the logic of the psyche. The enemy whom we force to wear the face of Death is a shadow puppet, a necessary part of the staging of our mortality-immortality play.

> *There is a type of soldier who considers death very real for others but without power over him. . . . They have simply preserved their childish illusion that they are the center of the world and therefore immortal.*
>
> Glenn Gray

U.S. as Death Casts a Shadow Over Spain
U.S.S.R.

In primitive mythology, death is considered an unnatural fact in need of explanation. It is not perceived as an inevitable consequence of being born. Death is accidental, exterior to human beings, not a part of our natural biological human destiny. It happens because we break a taboo of the gods, because we fail to obey the parents, the elders, the divine commandments. If we could only maintain our moral, physical, and ritual purity, we would be immortal. The final enemy—death—is potentially defeatable by the heroic psyche or nation who can follow the divine destiny without faltering.

Within each of us, intertwined with our will to live, is an *exigence for immortality.* It is not so much that we believe we are immortal as that we *demand* it regardless of whether our mind accepts or is embarrassed by the notion. It is only by some mental trick that we can even contemplate a world in which we are nonexistent. Orthodox Baptists and atheists alike demand their continuation beyond death in some symbolic form, whether in heaven, in their children, in the memory of friends, or in the institutions they have served. And because this near-instinctive exigence of immortality is balanced by the precariously repressed fear that death might really eradicate *all* traces of our existence, we are willing to go to any extreme to quiet our self-doubts and reassure ourselves. By submitting to the divine ordeal of war, in which we are willing to die or kill the enemy who *is* Death, we ritually affirm our own deathlessness. In its strongest or most literal form, this was reflected in the primitive propaganda that promised that the fallen warrior would go directly to Valhalla or Paradise. As recently as Vietnam, warriors proclaimed that they had already "served their time in hell." In its more sophisticated forms, it is still apparent in political funerals in which war heroes are buried in halls of fame where their memories will be preserved so long as men recount tales of courage and sacrifice.

The paradox of war, like that of iatrogenic medicine, is that it worsens the disease it promises to cure. Psychologically speaking, war is a project of those: (1) who refuse to believe in death; (2) who at the infantile level are nourished by the fantasy of their own immortality; and (3) who believe that by killing an enemy they can defeat death and prove themselves immortal. William Broyles, Jr., offers a vivid testimony to this fantasy:

> After one ambush my men brought back the body of a North Vietnamese soldier. I later found the

Flag: To Western Europe: Horse. Marshall plan. A rider with a fellow traveler
U.S.S.R.

The death fear of the ego is lessened by the killing, the sacrifice of others; through the death of the other, one buys oneself free from the penalty of dying, of being killed.
Otto Rank

dead man propped against some C-ration boxes. He had on sunglasses, and a *Playboy* magazine lay open in his lap; a cigarette dangled jauntily from his mouth, and on his head was perched a large and perfectly formed piece of shit. I pretended to be outraged, since desecrating bodies was frowned on as Un-American and counterproductive. But it wasn't outrage I felt. I kept my officer's face on, but inside I was . . . laughing. I laughed—I believe now—in part because of some subconscious appreciation of this obscene linkage of sex and excrement and death; and in part because of the exultant realization that he—whoever he had been—was dead and I—special, unique me—was alive. In war the line between life and death is gossamer thin; there is joy, pure joy, in being alive when so many around you are not. And from the joy of being alive in death's presence to the joy of causing death, is, unfortunately, not that great a step.

War as the bringer of death is Janus, two-faced. It wears the face of horror, but also of ecstacy. Soldiers often report that in spite of its brutality, war provided them with the most vivid experiences of their lives. Never were they more filled with awe and the precious, precarious, tragic sense of life. The constant atmosphere of danger, the felt potency of killing, the comradeship of men in arms, create a psychedelic high that releases the warrior from the quiet desperation and boredom of everyday life.

But perhaps if we look at warfare with the eye of the philosopher we may find that it is not, as it seems, a discipline of courage in the face of death so much as it is a desperate, black-magical effort to avoid dealing with the universal destiny of death. True enough, living in the presence of death is necessary for vividness. We lose our capacity for wonder and sink into boring routine when we conspire to forget the fragility of life and the closeness of death. As Heidegger said, we exist authentically only when we remember that we are beings-toward-death. To the extent that we repress the day-by-day awareness of our mortality, our death will go far from us and become hostile. And then we can reclaim it only in a perverse way by projecting it onto the face of the enemy, and trying to kill Death. Warfare is a perversion of our need to remember our mortality. It places men in a violent situation where they acknowledge death because they kill, not because they, like all

Uncle Sam with Abacus, Counting Bodies
U.S.S.R.

humans, are privileged to live only for a fleeting moment. Either we avoid death by becoming death killers, or we live with an awareness of the tragic sense of life. Philosophers, mystics, psychologists—the psychonauts who have dared to descend into the unconscious—have held out a strange promise: we can live fully and gently if we will daily remember our death. We become sensual, earthy, humble, by keeping in mind that fully human beings are humus—soil, fertile and decaying matter. D. H. Lawrence suggested as well as anyone the essential link between sexuality and the awareness of death when he called an orgasm "a gentle reaching out toward death." In love we cease trying to control, we give up the powergame, we experience ourselves as *with* rather than *against* the other, we declare an end to war. It is the testimony of the wisest that there is an ecstacy in ordinary life when warfare has ceased sufficiently to allow us to face death in a gentle way. To be human we must die. We need not kill.

THE STATISTICAL HUMAN

The Absence of Being

Scenario for the ultimate dehumanization: you look into the mirror and see no image at all. You have disappeared. Void.

The most frightening revelation we find in looking at ourselves in the mirror of the enemy is that we fear we have ceased to exist. The enemy is (we are) a statistic, an abstraction. In protest we cry out, "Call me any name you want, but do not render me anonymous. Curse me, but don't ignore me. Assign me any predicate, but don't deny that I am a subject. Portray me as an atheist or a beast, but not a cipher, a devil, but not a nonentity."

The void we seek to eradicate is ourselves. The enemy we have reduced to a body to be counted is the spirit of abstraction that has come to dominate the modern psyche. The numbered mass—100,000,000 or 200,000,000, give or take a few million—that might be eliminated in an initial nuclear exchange, is a symbol that we have become captured by a demonic quantification to the exclusion of quality. "How many?" "How much?" "How often?"—have become more important than "Why?" The means have triumphed over the ends. We have ceased to ask "Should we?" and ask only "Can we?"

**America as the abstract man,
interested only in numbers**
U.S.S.R.

Washington: *The Pentagon's latest
figure of enemy dead show July
5,500; August 5,860; and September 4,447. The monthly average for
these three months is 5,269. . . .
This works out to $322,000 spent
on every enemy soldier reported
killed.*
Louisville Courier-Journal, 12/18/66

*It is a freak of the times. We make
love by telephone, we work not on
matter but on machines, and we kill
and are killed by proxy.*
Albert Camus

Technology has brought in its wake a widespread destruction of the human spirit. Never have so many had
so much and felt so little. Affluence and nihilism have
gone hand in hand. Individualism has marched side by
side with anonymity and mass society. The more we
have been able to order and rationalize nature and society, the more the sense of anomie has increased. The
nearer we have come to being gods on earth, the less we
have felt human. With intelligence, imagination, and
industry, we have created the means to eliminate most
of the curse of hunger, infectious disease, poverty, ignorance, which were previously assumed to be an inevitable part of the human condition. Instead, we have
created surplus suffering.

In the most technologically advanced societies, the
majority lead highly regimented lives. Anonymous
bureaucracies, corporations, and governments control
where we live, work, are educated; whether and with
whom we fight, where we may travel, what we wear,
what we may say in public, what information we receive. The average person receives a standard diet of
advertising, forty hours a week of predigested television
entertainment and news.

Increasingly we are trained to be experts and professionals who can function only in highly specialized capacities. Of necessity, a mass-producing society reduces
the majority of workers to functionaries who must be
interchangeable with other functionaries. Worth is
measured by output. Everything conspires to standard-
ize consumer goods as well as consumer tastes. (With
appropriate differences in status and quality available
according to class and income: standard Mercedes for
the rich; standard Toyotas for the middle class; old
VW's for the poor.)

We are the anonymous people. We count only as abstractions, statistics. Our lives have been ruled by acci-
dents—being Jews, Arabs, Americans, Vietnamese. No
personal destiny has been strong enough to counteract
the great cipher makers. The important decisions are
not individual but corporate. Crown Zellerbach decides
to close the mill, and a thousand families must move.
We have progressed from machine, to statistic, to
nonentity. We don't belong in the category of person—
neither subhuman barbarians nor nonhuman animals.
We are not hated. Our elimination will be the result of
a computer-assisted decision, the logical conclusion of
a rational policy made with due consideration of alternative scenarios.

"I have improved on human rights. I have reduced the number of assassinations from 200 to 196. . . . You can count on us."
Roger. Nicaragua
© 1985 by Cartoonists and Writers Syndicate

It is little wonder that the essential human feeling of importance, meaning, significance, is being eroded. Psychiatrists report that the chief complaint of modern patients is depression: "Is this all there is?" Filled with food, conveniences, and entertainment, we nevertheless feel empty. In the wasteland, things are in the saddle and are riding us. And the emptiness, the boredom, the regimented depression festers, grows into free-floating anger, erupts into violence. The bottom line by which we assert our existence is not *Cogito ergo sum,* but "*I am violent, therefore I am.*" When we feel we don't count, aren't important, don't matter, violence becomes our last resource for crying: "I exist, I can make a difference, I am powerful." If we have lost the confidence that we can create anything that bears the stamp of our individual existence, respond to a calling by which we may earn a name for ourselves, we can still deny our impotence by destroying.

War has traditionally provided an adventure that is a temporary antidote for anomie and meaninglessness. The more orderly, controlled, and rationalized societies become, the more boredom becomes a problem. Modern workers are rewarded for being predictable and for tolerating routine. Apollo rules the corporate world. And it gets tedious. Middle management, no less than the masses, "live lives of quiet desperation," punctuated by the ritual violence of sports, 40,000 television murders per year, and war. When war comes, Dionysus escapes from his chains and runs wild. Men are called out of routine and thrust into strange lands where they may see and do exotic things. A year in Vietnam or Afghanistan is both a moral and esthetic holiday. The spice of danger adds intensity to every experience. Strange women excite eros, and the blood of enemies stimulates thanatos. *In extremis*, men touch the boundaries of love and death that are usually veiled in normal life.

And there is the intoxication of power. A nineteen-year-old, who in civilian life might be permitted the responsibility of driving a pizza delivery wagon, in battle commands a platoon and makes life and death decisions. His trigger finger is more potent to destroy life than anything within his yet-undeveloped personality is to create life.

Within this drama he is not alone, but a member of a "confraternity of danger." He fights with men he comes to love, and he knows "honor" and "sacrifice" not as abstractions, but as palpable experiences of risk and

INITIATIVE IN DEVELOPING NEW WEAPON SYSTEMS

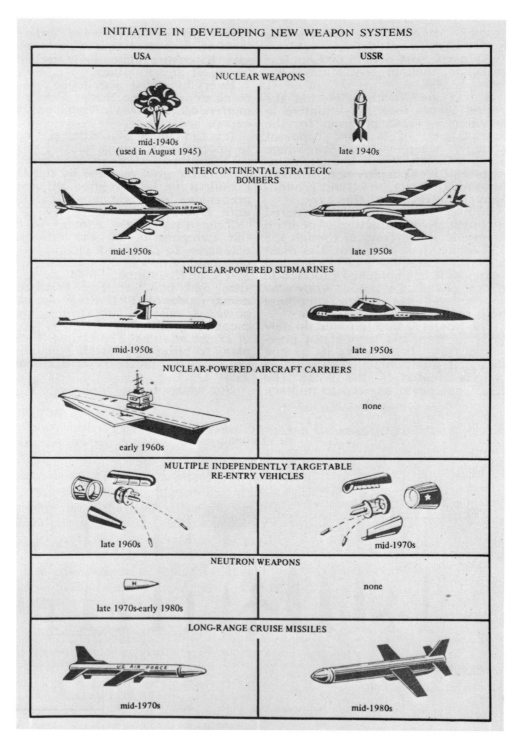

USA	USSR
NUCLEAR WEAPONS	
mid-1940s (used in August 1945)	late 1940s
INTERCONTINENTAL STRATEGIC BOMBERS	
mid-1950s	late 1950s
NUCLEAR-POWERED SUBMARINES	
mid-1950s	late 1950s
NUCLEAR-POWERED AIRCRAFT CARRIERS	
early 1960s	none
MULTIPLE INDEPENDENTLY TARGETABLE RE-ENTRY VEHICLES	
late 1960s	mid-1970s
NEUTRON WEAPONS	
late 1970s-early 1980s	none
LONG-RANGE CRUISE MISSILES	
mid-1970s	mid-1980s

**Whence the Threat to Peace?
"They started it."**
U.S.S.R., 1985

142

Mass Production

The U.S.A. *is* its weapons
U.S.S.R.

daring and the willingness to die for comrades. Few men in civilian life ever experience the dramatic intensity of war. Years afterward, even when the memory of the horror remains alive, many veterans nostalgically remember the most vivid years of their lives as their time of combat. Living in the presence of violence sets free in men both what is most bestial and what is most transcendent. Little wonder that many claim that battle for a man is the equivalent of childbirth for a woman. At no other time does a man by his suffering so dramatically stand on the border between life and death. The normal limits of everyday life that we so love and hate, are smashed in that festival of violence we call war. And who, but those in the throes of pain, can say that they are completely sorry to have their safe routines interrupted?

If, as we have claimed, propaganda is a coded message about ourselves, a revelation of our covert identity, the reduction of the enemy to a statistic that may be erased, along with ourselves, in a nuclear war, it tells us something both frightful and hopeful about the state of the modern human. A majority of us are alienated enough, empty enough, lacking in a *raison d'être* to be on the verge of suicide. In spite of our potential for material comfort, we have become problematic. Our deep, unconscious will to live is in danger. Our lives may not be rich enough in real meaning to make us want to survive. Freud suggested there is always a delicate balance between the forces of eros and thanatos in the human psyche. The conditions of modern life may be such that

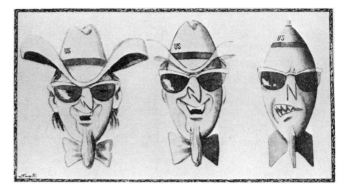

The human face of the U.S. is metamorphized into the Bomb
U.S.S.R.

There will be no peace until they have faces.

the balance has tipped and eros is threatened. When we make survival and prosperity depend on a psyche that has been toughened in order to compete, desensitized in order to conform, and emptied of feeling in order to destroy, we create a spiritual ecology in which eros cannot flower.

If the escalating anonymity and hostility of modern life is cause for despair, it is also an invitation to hope. As Camus reminded us a generation ago, authentic choice only emerges when we are willing to look at the absurd. Neither potent action nor hope can arise out of technological optimism or evolutionary idealism that assumes we are automatically progressing toward a magical transformation of human beings and a golden "new age." Both individuals and nations sometimes reach a point of disenchantment with life where they commit suicide. There is no more dangerous or hopeful moment than when we dare to hold the possibility of life and death in our hands and ask, "To be or not to be?" That is the point we have reached in human history. After millennia of struggle and triumph, we have finally reached the moment when we have the power and the necessity to decide whether to die or to change. Either we become the ultimate enemy, the devil who destroys humanity, or we assert our potency and will to create a future unlike our past, a future not dominated by *Homo hostilis*.

PART 3

THE FUTURE OF ENMITY

A Potpourri of Possibilities

The human future depends on whether we can cease inventing more ingenious means for destroying our enemies and create social institutions that will lessen our enmity.

CREATING THE FUTURE

The Sweet Burden of Freedom

Imagine the vanity of thinking your enemy can do you more harm than your enmity.
Augustine

Realism demands that we begin any speculation about the future with the bleakest scenarios. If we extrapolate the major trends of the twentieth century, it is likely there will be a nuclear holocaust. Nationalism, the warrior psyche, progress in weapons technology, and the habit of projecting our shadows onto our enemies all add up to a near-certain formula for disaster. Humanity may not survive. The mythological "heroes" who best reflect our species may turn out to be, first, Prometheus, who stole the fire from the gods and was chained to a rock and cursed to have his liver consumed by a vulture for his hubris; and, second, Satan, the fallen angel who worshipped power.

Pessimists take a grim delight, optimists an easy comfort, in determinism. For both, the outcome of history is already written and all we have to do is sit back and await the final act. For the pessimists the selfish gene and the logic of power politics condemn us to perpetual, and therefore final, war. For the optimist, the secret unfolding of the evolution of matter-becoming-spirit will inevitably lead to a transformation of human society and a New Age.

Armaggedon or utopia? A destiny programmed by biology or spirit?

Neither. The perspective from which I will play with the possible futures is the belief in *freedom*. We are neither condemned by our genes nor saved from the folly we choose by a *deus ex machina*. We must refuse the metaphysical pride of both secular and religious forms of predestination. "The fault . . . lies not in our stars, but in ourselves, that we are underlings" (Shakespeare, *Julius Ceasar*). And being underlings means nothing more than the refusal to bear the sweet burden of our freedom. Rather than suffer the creative anxiety of potent freedom, we deify the nation and manufacture all the easy comforts of mass religion and ritual war. Then we tranqualize ourselves with pious political rhetoric that assures us that we have no alternative because "the enemy" forces us to defend ourselves. Such rationaliza-

146

**German Militarism as
Frankenstein**
W.W.I

James J. Dobbins

tions are the essence of "bad faith." Whether we accept the secular formulation of an existentialist such as Sartre that "we are condemned to be free" or the mystic affirmation that our freedom is the most tangible evidence we have that we are created by a loving God, we must begin all authentic thought about the future standing on the rock of freedom. We are free; therefore we have the responsibility to create. The story of the future of enmity is not yet written. Not by god, destiny, technology, power politics, nor the DNA. We remain human in the measure that we accept responsibility.

There is no single scenario for the future of enmity. Our speculation and prevision must be in the subjunctive mood: *perhaps, maybe, suppose, if this, then that, what if, let's pretend, it is as if.* The reason most predictions about the future are boring is because they are predicated on the view that the story is already finished. But the future is *not* fact, but fantasy. Therefore let us play with what we might yet become.

U.S.S.R., W.W.II

The boundaries within which our game will be played are the opposite unthinkable (but possible) conditions: 1) Absolute enmity triumphs and we destroy all human life; 2) we recreate society and the psyche in such a way as to end the long habit of enmity. We will play with possibilities for reducing enmity that lie between these two extremes of oblivion and total love.

Should our approach to the lessening of enmity be on the polis or the psyche? On short-term or long-term changes? Both. In the short term we need to find emergency measures. Granted, war is a symptom of a more fundamental disease. We must treat the symptom to keep the patient alive long enough to discover how to

Never Again
John Heartfield. DDR, 1960

To discover the true enemy, the holy war, the good fight: Shift your eyes. Expand your focus from the local to the universal, from the particular to the general, from the national enemy to the human enemy.

change the social and political ecology that creates the disease. Short of transforming the psyche, we must negotiate the conditions that will allow *Homo hostilis* to live in that state of conflict that has been the definition of normality for the past 13,000 years. It would be an advancement over our present situation of absolute danger if we could return to the relative dangers of traditional warfare. But eventually we must face the nearly unimaginable task of transforming the warrior psyche, or ending the long tyranny of enmity, of discovering what William James called "the moral equivalent of war."

In this final section I will raise some questions and sketch some possibilities for both emergency and eventual treatments for the disease of enmity.

MINIMAL SOLUTIONS

Desperate Hopes

Must we decide between being dead-right or dead-wrong?

Hope is a mustard seed. It grows better in sparse land than in utopia. Something about beginning with the bare minimum nourishes radical honesty. Let's start with honest despair. Perhaps we have little power or will to reverse the suicidal course of *Homo hostilis*. If so, our freedom may be reduced to the desperate choice of dying well, rather than poorly. If we are now standing together on the deck of the *Titanic*, we may at least sing as it sinks.

In playing with alternative visions of the future of enmity, I will begin with the least desirable and minimal solutions and escalate to the most desirable maximal political solutions, and beyond that to the radical solutions that depend on a transformation of the psyche and the polis.

The minimalist solutions are based on the assumption that we neither examine nor change our images of the enemy as absolute evil and the policies that are based on this assumption. Since the possibility of intentional change is always in direct proportion to the quantity of trust, this option offers little chance of change. If the enemy is inhuman and completely untrustworthy, the search for armed superiority is a reasonable course of action.

The minimal solutions are, of course, inadequate and absurd. But, alas, it is not clear that humankind would rather save its life than lose its paranoia. We may prefer to die angry than to live with the kind of radical trust necessary to create rational and compassionate policies.

The Cyanide Kool-Aid Scenario

Assumption: Enmity and technology continue their trajectory. And weapons accumulated will eventually be used. Full-scale nuclear war between the United States and the U.S.S.R. breaks out. The effects, as scientists have predicted, are immediate genocide and the beginning of a nuclear winter. Few, if any, will survive in either country.

Proposal: Insofar as this is possible and even probable, given the current unwillingness on the part of either the United States or the U.S.S.R. to undertake the type of radical political changes necessary to avert nuclear war, the governments of each country should agree to end the cruel hoax of "civil defense" and issue

Nelson Harding. U.S. 1927
Courtesy of Brooklyn Public Library,
Eagle Collection

U.S.S.R., Pravda

cyanide capsules to the head of every family. The worst possible thing any of us can imagine is *not* dying immediately at ground zero of a nuclear explosion. My most horrible nightmare is of having to bludgeon my wife and children to death in the advanced stages of radiation poisoning. The governmental leaders of nations with nuclear arsenals on their soil have assumed the same stance as Rev. Jim Jones in Guyana. They have convinced their followers they must be prepared to die, to commit suicide, and perhaps cosmocide, in order to save themselves from being taken over by an enemy who destroys both body and soul. If we are to continue a strategy of nuclear deterrence in which all civilian populations are held hostage, we should be willing to be lucid and candid about the worst-case and provide our citizens with the cyanide and Kool-Aid necessary to die with a minimum of dignity.

The Bubonic Exchange

Assumption: The United States and the U.S.S.R. reach an agreement that, although they are absolute enemies, in the event of their mutual suicide through warfare, the nonhuman world need not be destroyed. Both agree that isolated pockets of people who are not involved in the ideological death struggle between communism and capitalism should survive and continue the human experiment.

Proposal: All nuclear warheads should immediately be replaced by chemical agents, such as bubonic plague, botulism, or nerve gas that would be immediately fatal to humans but not other animals. In a world where evil has all but triumphed, it is significantly more moral to commit mass murder than cosmocide, to limit the effect of war to the guilty species—humans. Such a strategy would allow us to continue our suicidal arms race but allow us to preserve the slight consolation that in our absence the deer and the antelope might continue to play. The human experiment is, in the geological time frame, relatively recent. In a million years or so (a figure that should seem small in comparison to our military budgets), the monkeys might breed a new Adam who would have sense enough to stay in the Garden.

An important side effect of adopting the bubonic alternative is that we could switch our military research from the useless quest for more horrible explosive weapons and concentrate on creating disease entities and antidotes. Instead of an arms race, we would have a toxin and immunization race, Gene Wars rather than Star Wars, recombinant DNA rather than particle-beam weapons. Although medical research is not without social hazards it is, without argument, likely to produce more knowledge that is useful in overcoming suffering than is weapons research.

It is also possible that some individuals would prove to have unique immunities to the worst biological weapons created. Thus, whatever survivors were left after the Bubonic Exchange would begin to create a race from a biologically superior genetic strain. (In the best of all possible scenarios—the Sadist Sanction—we would invent a biological agent that would destroy only the most hostile and aggressive, and would leave the meek to inherit the earth.)

The Survivalist Scenario

Assumption: A limited nuclear war breaks out between the U.S. and the U.S.S.R. Instead of triggering the Doomsday machine, we pause in the middle of the madness and restrain our second-strike capacity. Or a majority of our missiles simply fail to function. Since

War is The Enemy.

152

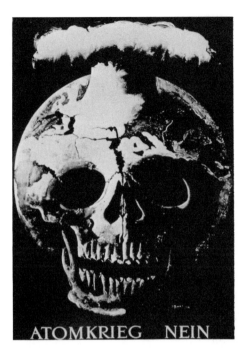

Atomic War
Hans Erni. Germany, 1954
By personal permission

WINGS OVER EUROPE.

WEDNESDAY, MAY 15, 1940.

Fitzpatrick. St. Louis Post-Dispatch
W.W.II

the policy of Mutual Assured Destruction was followed, each side targeted, held hostage, and destroyed the large population centers.

Proposal: If we assume that reason might prevail in chaos when it did not in calm, and that a nuclear war might be limited to casualties of a few hundred million, then massive civil defense programs should be instituted. Self-contained survivalist communities with the essential technological knowledge, humanistic wisdom, and artistic skills capable of reseeding a new civilization should be sprinkled in remote rural areas. Many of the science fiction stories that play with such a theme stress that it may take a semitotal nuclear war to finally educate the mass of people to the futility of seeking military solutions to problems.

The Proliferation Game

Assumption: Dualism *is* warfare. A world composed of two competing powers is more dangerous than one

M.A.D.—MEN. (Mutual Assured Destruction.)

composed of a multiplicity of competing powers. As Milton Rokeach illustrated in *Three Christs of Ipsilanti*, several madmen in a room are more likely to arrive at a reasonable solution than two madmen in a room. Power corrupts, but so does powerlessness. By the end of the century, any nation that cares to will be able to manufacture nuclear arms. Since a small arsenal of nuclear weapons is all that is necessary to enter into the big-league game of blackmail deterrence politics, we will see an equalization of power between small and large nations. Just as a Colt .45 was the equalizer in the last century, the Cruise Missile is the equalizer in the twentieth century. Everybody gets one vote about Armaggedon. And, unless the vote is unanimous, the war begins.

Army Medical Examiner: "At last a perfect soldier."
Robert Minor. The Masses. U.S., 1916

Headless Generals
U.S.S.R.

Proposal: Insofar as our strategy has been to create more and more destructive weapons as "bargaining chips" to get the enemy to agree to arms limitation, let us carry the policy to its logical conclusion and offer nuclear technology to any nation that requests it, to hasten the possibility of world disarmament. We will, thereby, increase the danger so radically that the major world powers will be forced to cooperate to create a universal nuclear disarmament, or else they will lose their status as major powers. So long as we play the game of pure power politics, which may be stated with some apology to Clausewitz as "power comes out of the barrel of a gun," our best hope is that the balance of terror might move us toward a more stable world. Nations possessing the nuclear equalizer would likely move toward greater economic equality and thus lessen the economic causes of war.

If this proposal seems somewhat bizarre, consider the madcap logic on which our present policy is based. Current attempts to retain a nuclear monopoly and to prevent "proliferation," is the late-twentieth-century version of paternalism and colonialism. We assume that countries such as Libya and Iraq are not politically mature enough to use nuclear weapons in a reasonable way. If, as we all assume, military power is the only guarantor of sovereignty, then the most reasonable way to ensure the sanctity of national boundaries is to give all nations the wherewithal to defend their territory against aggressors. If the United States had kindly offered Tibet and Afghanistan a few minimegaton warheads, and the U.S.S.R. offered a similar selection of equalizers to the Viet Cong or the Sandinistas, the world might be far more dangerous, or much safer. Supposedly, the immature only become mature by becoming responsible for the management of power. So the world won't grow up until all nations have the means for committing cosmocide. At that point we can expect the developing nations of the Third World to be as responsible as the most developed nations have become.

The People's Peace Zone Plan

Assumption: Most people seem to agree that it is governments and leaders and not "the people" who want war. As a condition of minimal civility, the nuclear powers agree that in warfare they want to destroy only the guilty and not the innocent.

Proposal: The major world powers convene a new Geneva Convention and agree that the concept of chivalry should be reintroduced into warfare, that battle should be limited to the exchange of hostilities among professional military men, and that innocent civilians should no longer be used as hostages.

Each nation should divide its territory between war and peace zones. All military personnel, their families, major government offices, weapons, and the military-industrial complex, should be located in the war zone.

Unless we discover civility and create new institutions to tame our greed and gentle our anger, every advance in technology will bring us nearer to barbarism and cosmocide.

U.S., W.W.II

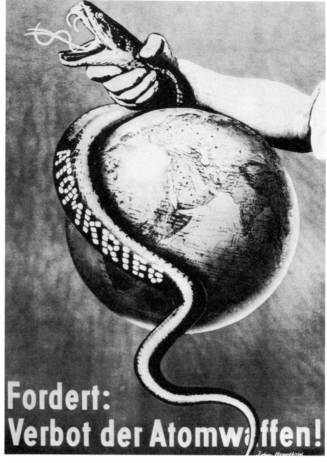

It is necessary to prohibit atomic weapons.
John Heartfield. DDR, 1955

All nonmilitary persons, economy, and culture, should be concentrated in peace zones. All conventional and nuclear warfare should take place only in designated war zones. Such a division would allow people to choose what type of culture they prefer. Although the risk of living in the war zone would be greater, its economy would be richer, due to the concentration of defense spending, and its inhabitants more affluent. It would also eliminate all problems about verification and cheating on arms control, because no nation could object to its arms-free zones being open for inspection.

Such a plan might lead automatically, in the long run, to world peace. By a process of natural selection, inhabitants in the war zone would be those possessing the qualities that are essential for the warrior psyche—aggression, single-mindedness, authoritarianism, capacity to endure regimentation, love of combat, desire for power, extroversion, unconscious projection of hostility onto the enemy and so on. Inevitably war would be a regular occurrence between those dwelling in respective war zones and thus their numbers would decrease. They might, conceivably, eliminate each other in a nuclear duel, leaving as survivors those human being who had opted to live in the peace zones.

MODERATE SOLUTIONS

Civilized Hostilities

Each step in this escalating series of moderate solutions is predicated on a renunciation of the notion of holy wars and absolute enemies, an increasing trust level, and ability to become conscious and self-critical about one's own capacity for creating surplus evil. We must say both yes and no to the enemy. We stand *against* you but also *with* you. Together we form a community of competing nations, a commonwealth of civil hostility and our social contract is to create the conditions that will allow us to continue our competition.

Moderate solutions are based on the belief that the major part of conflicts between nations is caused by misunderstanding, and that the antidote is increasing communication and understanding. Most of these scenarios ultimately rest on the Socratic faith that might be stated something like this:

> To know the good is to do the good.
> Ignorance of our enemies blinds us to the common good.
> To know our enemies is to do the common good.

Rhetorical Civility: Playing the China Card

Assumption: In the beginning is the word. How we name a thing, a person, or a nation, shapes our perception and conduct. Poetry is the most practical art; our metaphors determine our practice. Politics is stuck in the repetition of bad metaphors. The warrior psyche is imprisoned by the metaphor of power. Power politics is a litany that may bore us to death. Fundamental changes in politics no less than in physics or personal

157

**Question.
And answer?**

relations begin in perceptual shifts. The circuit of transformation goes from metaphor, to rhetoric, to action; from seeing, to saying, to doing.

The single largest impediment to keeping the world safe enough for limited conflict is absolute rhetoric.

Jack Tar (England) fighting Buonaparte. 1798.

One does not reason with devils. Against the enemies of God, nothing less than a righteous crusade is appropriate. If we must be dead right, and the enemy dead wrong, we will both be dead—right or wrong. We need human enemies with whom we can contend, not subhuman or suprahuman enemies who must be eliminated.

Proposal: We plan and carry out a campaign of rhetorical de-escalation in which the dehumanizing language of propaganda is replaced by metaphors that dignify the enemy.

The prime example we have in recent times of the success of this strategy is the change in U.S.-China relations that began with Nixon's visit. Diplomatic dinners with toasts to friendship, the exploration of trading possibilities, and the exchange of ping-pong teams accompanied the tearing down of wall posters picturing the United States as a "paper dragon" or a "running

C. D. Batchelor. N.Y. Daily News. 1936

U.S., W.W. II

dog" of imperialism. When Dr. Paul Dudley White observed operations in which the patients were anesthetized by the ancient technique of acupuncture, Americans began to be fascinated with China. Suddenly our enemy was not a faceless yellow horde, but a civilized person who cultivated the arts, sought to make a reasonable blend between ancient and modern medicine, took care to preserve the panda bear. Coca Cola and capitalism established a beachhead in China with nary a shot fired.

Lest unrepentant realists miss the point, this remarkable change from enmity to friendship was not based on any significant change in the distribution of power. Afterward as before, China remained a communist nation with territorial ambitions and a supporter of national liberation armies. As a condition of friendship, we did not demand that they cease the systematic armed repression and occupation of their neighbor Tibet, an action every bit as barbaric as the Soviet's invasion of Afghanistan. From rhetoric and ceremony, we moved rapidly into greater cultural exchange and trade and a more civilized conversation about how to live with each other.

The Knowledge Gap: Knowing Our Enemy

Assumptions: In the present situation, it is not the biblical injunction to love our enemies we must heed so much as the strategic demand that we know our enemy. Paranoia and propaganda so cloud perception that neither the United States nor the U.S.S.R. understands the motives or national psyche of the other. Americans who have never seen a Soviet are in charge of weapons systems that might exterminate an entire people. To stop the inevitable slide toward war we must now consciously fill the knowledge gap and create a new image of our enemy. As enemies, the U.S. and the U.S.S.R. need to move sufficiently close to become real to each other. Like good samurai swordsmen, we need to be interested enough in our opponents to know whether and how to fight effectively. We need not go further and adopt the sentimental philosophy that "to know them is to love them." A known enemy is not necessarily a friend. It would be foolish for Americans to ignore the bloody history of Soviet self-repressions—the purges of Stalin, the Gulags, the continuing thought control—or the commitment of Marxism to world conquest in the name of eliminating class exploitation, or their repressive hold over Eastern Europe. Just as it would be foolish for Soviets to ignore the racial injustice, the radical inequalities between rich and poor, the destructive consumerism, the bloody efforts to impose "democracy" on Vietnam and Nicaragua that are products of American capitalism. Daring to know each other's vices and virtues, we will become ambivalent rather than absolute enemies. And that would make the world considerably safer.

Proposal: We should do everything possible to increase student exchange, tourism, exchange of children and grandchildren of high governmental and military officers, citizen diplomacy, professional association, and all forms of direct communication. We need to use satellite link-ups that will allow citizens of each country to talk directly to each other. Several of these "space bridges" have already been created that permitted live

U.S. Defense Department

studio audiences in Los Angeles and Moscow to share music and ask questions of each other. Plans for sister cities to engage in a regular program of meetings via satellite are now underway. The current agreement to allow *Soviet Life* magazine to be circulated in the U.S. and the American equivalent in the U.S.S.R. should be extended to create a permanent open television channel on which Soviets could present their point of view directly to American audiences and vice versa. An obvious problem with this proposal is that the present Soviet system does not allow the press to criticize foreign policy and that American media, while having the freedom to investigate and criticize, takes little interest in Soviet life beyond presenting stereotypes. If we posited an atmosphere of moderate trust, both nations would strengthen their social systems and lessen the risk of accidental war by increasing communication.

Mutual Crisis Control Center

Assumption: Many wars start by accident. An archduke is assassinated, or a flight of Canada Geese on a radar screen is mistaken for hostile incoming missiles, and an irrevocable decision to go to war is made.

Moreover, superpowers and nation-states are also often drawn into regional conflicts in which they have no strategic interest by a principle of hostile linkage (any enemy of our enemy is an ally of ours).

Proposal: The United States and the U.S.S.R. (and other symbiotic enemies) set up joint crisis centers staffed with high-level military and political personnel who would guard against war by accident. Such small centers, which were in fact proposed to the U.S. Congress by Senator Jackson, could also work out agreements of restraint in which we would mutually agree not to supply arms or intervene in certain regional conflicts such as the Iran-Iraq War. It would seem to require a minimum of restraint for the United States and the U.S.S.R. to de-escalate their involvement and agree not to supply arms in Central America, the Caribbean, Africa, and the Middle East.

Arms Limitations

Assumption: Within the limits of the present demand of sovereign nations, power politics, and national enmity, it is still possible to moderate our risks of both the possibility and the destructive consequences of war.

Missile Envy.
© Lou Myers, U.S.
Used by special permission.

A further assumption is that a phased nuclear disarmament, even if the process must be started unilaterally, poses no real threat to national security, since our overkill capacity is so enormous.

Proposal: As George Kennan, our former ambassador to the U.S.S.R., has suggested, the United States should take moral leadership by challenging the Soviets to run the arms race backwards and begin a phased destruction of nuclear weapons. To show our good faith, we should unilaterally, if necessary, destroy one-half of our nuclear arsenal. The remaining half would still be sufficient to maintain a credible deterrent against any threat of Soviet attack. Whatever risks there might be in such a reduction are less than the risks of an unrestrained arms race. Currently nuclear weapons function as a Catch-22 deterrent: They are credible only if the enemy believes we will use them; but we all know, as Tom Lehrer said, "We will all go together when we go." In this situation of mutually agreed delusion, very few weapons are needed to maintain the Doomsday threat.

U.S.S.R.

Kevin Kallaugher. England
© 1985 by Cartoonists and Writers Syndicate

The Armless Race: Humanizing Conflict

Assumptions: The conflicts between the United States and the U.S.S.R. and between the developed and underdeveloped nations, are substantial and not likely to be dissolved by better understanding. How society is organized and who gets what share of the resources is at stake. However, the present situation where the United States and the U.S.S.R. have become the arms merchants and munitions suppliers and have, thus, militarized almost all conflicts, is counterproductive for all concerned.

Proposal: The United States and the U.S.S.R. agree to fight their ideological war for the hearts and minds, trade agreements, natural resources, and alignment, with nonmilitary weapons. Let each nation send as many doctors, engineers, teachers, propagandists, experts of one kind or another (and highly paid philosophers), to any nation that requests aid. But no arms. The rule of the game of unarmed combat is "Whoever resorts to violence admits philosophical defeat." This most humane form of bloodless warfare is the best alternative short of restructuring nation-states to eliminate warfare. It recognizes the seriousness of conflict, the crucial differences between enemies, but it humanizes the weapons. The beauty of such a solution is that the United States and the U.S.S.R. could negotiate and agree to try such an experiment in some part of the world where they are now peripherally involved without having first to change the nuclear deterrence game. Conceivably the trust created by a limited experiment in restraint might spread.

MAXIMAL SOLUTIONS

Limited Sovereignty and World Law

Obstacles to ending war:

1. The belief that war is rooted in human nature and cannot be eradicated
2. The belief that nuclear deterrence can be maintained indefinitely
3. The belief that the Soviet Union cannot be challenged and turned from an expansionistic course by anything other then military power
4. The belief that nationalism, or cultural or religious differences, pose insurmountable barriers

Robert Woito

The maximal political solution to the problem of war will require an evolutionary step comparable to the enlargement of loyalty and sense of membership and in-group loyalty that took place in the transition from the tribe to the nation. In its early stages, nationalism limited hostility by creating a metatribal identity. We are now faced with the necessity to create a metanational identity. This effort will require an enormous shift in which we limit national sovereignty and transfer effective military and political power to some world peace-keeping force.

The maximal scenarios for world peace are based on the assumption that wars are not caused primarily by a lack of understanding and communication, but by the differing interests of sovereign nations. In our present situation of nationalistic anarchy, we have no effective world law. War is "the continuation of policy by other means."[30] And there is no realistic way to stop it without providing some metanational political body with the power to adjudicate national conflicts. Sooner or later we must either so transform the psyche that we lose the defense mechanisms that lead us to project our enmity, or face the necessity of taking the next step in political evolution beyond nationalism.

There are many steps, some already taken, that lead in this direction. After our first two World Wars, we attempted to jump into a League of Nations and a United Nations. But in each case the most powerful nations

U.S.S.R.

De La Torre. Columbia,
© 1983 by Cartoonists and Writers Syndicate

were not willing to limit their sovereignty (that is, their "right" to use unilateral violence) and to create an army sufficiently independent and strong to enforce the incipient rule of world law. It may require a third World War with near-total destruction before the survivors will be willing to give up their addiction to sovereign anarchy.

An interim step might be the divestment of empires by the major powers. As Patricia Ellsberg observed, the United States and the U.S.S.R. do not fear each other so much as they fear the loss of what is not justly theirs—their empires. It is not the threat to our borders that has created the arms race but a bloated sense of national interest, a self-image without boundaries.

At first glance it seems unlikely that the superpowers would be willing to divest themselves of their empires. But history shows us clearly that empires are notoriously unstable. In our time we have seen the beginning of the end of the old colonialism, the collapse of the British and the French empires. Empires are increasingly difficult to maintain. Keeping the far-flung boundaries safe from enemies systematically depletes the center. The more one must control, the greater the inevitability that chaos, rebellion, and resistance will occur. As Hegel saw clearly, in the master-slave relationship the master is as bound as the slave. Trying to maintain the illusion of control is exhausting.

Eventually the cost of weapons and of maintaining military empires, which require internal repression of freedom and the draining of resources needed for domestic prosperity, may force the superpowers to move toward divestment. It may be cost-effective for a number of years to exploit the resources of a colony, but the rising tide of nationalism and the demand for self-determination eventually make the price of trying to maintain control too high. Politically there is a principle that parallels Nietzsche's announcement that God is dead. The idea of a single organizing center, a hierarchy with God, the King, the President, or the Commissar at the apex, is a holdover from the medieval theological world view. It cannot long withstand the modern paradigm that has discovered that the organization necessary to sustain the universe is present in each particle of matter. What modern physics has shown us is that the center is everywhere. Reality is locally governed. The unity that binds the parts together is invisible. Totalitarian political organizations, like the old-fashioned God, topple from their own weight. Occasionally nations

I do not know the limits of the possible.

Kevin Kallaugher. England
© 1985 by Cartoonists and Writers Syndicate

What would you sacrifice to end war?

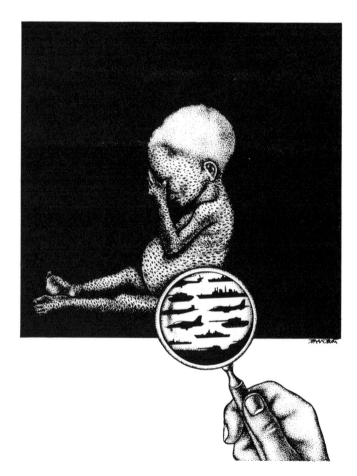

Vlahovic. Jugoslavia
© 1985 by Cartoonists and Writers Syndicate

have the sense to divest themselves gracefully of the empires that are not justly theirs and pull back within more limited and defensible boundaries. Our real national interest is to make the world safe for plurality.

The obvious first step necessary to any lasting solution of the war problem is a decision to create a body of world law, a world court, and a world army. We need not posit some world government in which nations renounce autonomy over what goes on within their borders. No sane person wants to see a world bureaucracy that tries to manage local affairs from a centralized command center. But no major change can occur in the war system until nations are willing to limit their sovereignty at one crucial point—the right to exercise violence outside of their own boundaries. Effective arms control means that all nations must possess nothing but defensive weapons. All nuclear weapons sufficient to destroy an entire nation, which might therefore be a sufficient deterrent to aggression, must be in the sole possession of a world army, under the jurisdiction of a world court that is committed to enforce world law.

In the long run, this "impossible dream" is probably the only realistic political scenario for limiting warfare in a way that will permit human survival.

RADICAL SOLUTIONS

The Struggle Against Enmity

The radical approach to enmity is based on the following assumptions:

1. The human species is very young. Our social evolution has just begun. Nature, Life, Evolution, or God—pick your belief system—is not yet finished with us. Therefore the past is not an accurate mirror in which to find an adequate reflection of human possibilities.

2. The real enemy against which we must struggle is the war system. This system includes both the political institutions through which we educate and habituate ourselves to war and the psychological defense mechanisms of *Homo hostilis*.

3. An immediate impediment to ending war is the mind set, the myth of *Homo hostilis*, which convinces us *a priori* that war is inevitable and any hope of a world without war is utopian.

4. Should we be willing to tamper with our beliefs and consider war an optional social institution, we might well be able to eliminate many of the concrete factors—social injustice, poverty, ignorance—that, realistically speaking, are causes of war.

5. The new mode of heroism that can and should replace the ancient reverence for the warrior and the heroic sacrifice for and in war, could focus on the breathtaking possibility of creating a new ideal—*Homo amicus* (Homomulier amicalus), the kindly human. This will require both a new polis and a new psyche. The courage to think of this possibility is the first step in its realization.

6. The first necessity is a new vision, a philosophical-theological-attitudinal breakthrough, a new sense of possibility. From this vision will flow new ways of acting, new institutions, new ways of minimizing conflict.

Fritz Behrendt. Netherlands
© 1985 by Cartoonists and Writers Syndicate

De La Torre. El Espectador. Colombia.
© 1984 by Cartoonists and Writers Syndicate.

WAR
AS
A
SOCIAL
INVENTION

The choice is simple, Utopia or the war now being prepared by antiquated modes of thought.

Albert Camus

To play with the notion of radical solutions is to assume that war has been invented as a means both to give our lives a particular type of mythic meaning and as a way of settling our differences of opinion.

If we are to find new solutions, we must take responsibility for our past creations. So long as we play the victim game ("It just happens to us"), the blame game ("Our enemies made us do it"), or the God game ("We do it for God"), we will lack both the vision and the potency to change. We must begin by giving up simplistic views and studying the complexities of the war system. As modern physics has moved from an atomic to a quantum view of matter, from particle to connecting web, and modern psychotherapy has moved from an emphasis on the individual to the family system and the social context, so must modern theory about war move from the single explanations (whether political, theological, psychological, or economic) to an examination of the intricate dance that goes on between enemies. We need to chart the "adversarial symbiosis," the complex social institutions, and the process of mystification of power and authority that are necessary to create and

Tony Auth. © Washington Post Writers Group
Used by special permission

Boardman Robinson. U.S. W.W.I

sustain the warrior psyche and the habit of war. It is naive to think that war will disappear simply because we want it to, because we have more terrible weapons that might create carnage on a yet-unimaginable scale. The folly of war has never been avoided in the past because of reason or goodwill. Any real alternative to war will be as intricate and complex, and will require the invention of as many new social institutions, as were designed to support the old war system. Our only hope of a lasting solution is radical.

War may be a disease, but it is the best way we have found as yet to do a number of things that we value. As every physician or psychotherapist knows, people very often get attached to their diseases not because they love suffering, but because they get "secondary gains" from illness. It makes them important; they are cared for by others; they are forced to rest, retire, retreat from stress, to make life changes they would not otherwise make; the life-death drama serves as a rite of passage in which they demonstrate their courage and emerge reborn, and so on. As an intricately institutionalized invention, warfare serves needs that must be satisfied. If we are serious about ending this ancient social disease, we must design ways in which the social and psychological needs, no less than the political functions that it satisfies in a perverted way, may be met in a more healthful manner.

HONORABLE EQUIVALENTS OF WAR

On Loving Combat

I have deliberately swerved away from the much-quoted and little-explored formulation of William James, "the moral equivalents of war." In a healthy-minded and robust manner, James suggested a rational equivalent of war. He wanted us to preserve a military character with its hardihood, discipline, manly disdain of ease and pleasure, intrepidity, contempt of softness, surrender of private interest, obedience to command, by creating a kind of Peace Corps. He suggested that by military conscription of youth we might form an army against nature that would also serve to create wealth that could be shared by the poor:

> To coal and iron mines, to freight trains, to fishing fleets in December, to dish-washing, clothes-washing, and window-washing, to road-building and tunnel-making, to boundaries and stoke-holes, and to the frames of skyscrapers, would our gilded youths be drafted off, and according to their choice, to get the childishness knocked out of them, and to come back into society with healthier sympathies and soberer ideas. They would have paid their blood-tax, done their own part in the immemorial human warfare against nature, would

treat the earth more proudly, the women would value them more highly, they would be better fathers and teachers of the following generation.[31]

In the years since James wrote, we have come to see war as a more complex and systemic problem. If the future of enmity is to be different than its past, we must

The Fruit of Red Education
Germany, pre-W.W.II

De La Torre. Columbia
© 1985 by Cartoonists and Writers Syndicate

think not merely of rational or moral equivalents, but of theological, psychological, political, erotic, economic, dramatic, educational, entertainment, ritual equivalents of war. Since we have already traced some of the political alternatives in discussing the maximal solutions, we will turn now to the social and psychological dimensions of the problem.

BEYOND THE GOD OF WAR

The Rebirth of Purpose

In war each nation worships itself.

It is impossible to think about the future of enmity and alternatives to war without beginning with theology. "God" has been the linchpin in the war system, the guardian spirit of tribes and nations, the transcendent sanction for genocide. In large measure, institutional religion has been a support for the ego and the ideology of society. The Lord of Hosts, the mighty man of war, has been the God of the realm—*Gott mit uns*—the God in whom we trust to keep our ramparts and economies strong. This God, the secretary of defense, has for generations been urging onward Christian, Jewish, and Muslim soldiers, trampling out the vintage where the grapes of wrath are stored, not averse to dashing little ones' heads against stones to protect the holy land. Lately he has been deciding whether to usher in the year 2000 with Armaggedon, not without the help of nuclear weapons, star wars, and one president who takes biblical prophecy seriously and another who takes Marxist prophecy seriously. This war God is a vampire who thrives on blood, is the agent of disharmony between nations, the sanctifier of personal and political paranoia.

For all the suffering he has caused, he has given us a *raison d'être*, a purpose, a transcendent destiny. So long as we have killed our neighbors in his name, we have been certain of our divine calling. It was he who gave America a "manifest destiny," granted Britain the dignity of bearing "the white man's burden," allowed the Japanese to create a Greater East Asia Co-Prosperity Sphere, helped Mussolini to rebuild the glorious Roman Empire, and prompted Hitler to envision the thousand-year Reich. Recently he has been active on both sides of the Irish civil wars. He has slain his thousands in new holy wars in Israel, Lebanon, Iran, and Iraq.

Nothing novel, kind, or hopeful can be created in the future unless we kill off this God, the idol of the tribe, unless we cease offering our blood to Moloch.

The basis of a new social order is a theological revolution.

This revolution begins with two major destructive tasks, two negations, two prophetic no's:

The first no is to the state. Religion must be *dis*established. The traditional link between church and state needs to be broken. Even if we have to be silent for a generation, the name "God" must no longer be used as

To find the true war, the true sacrament; to avoid idolatry—To see the sacrment of war as a false sacrament, is to see the demonic parody, the anti-Christ.

N. O. Brown

the sanctifier of carnage. Theology should deny the body politic its easy conscience. The notion that nations have a cosmic destiny and may therefore sanctify the use of violence is too dangerous an idea to continue to entertain. A truly secular state, which must bear responsibility for its policies and justify them in secular terms, is far less dangerous than a messianic state. National theologies are idolatrous. Before we can create an effective transnational theology, we need the sacred no of a thousand prophetic voices that refuse to allow the name of God to be used in partisan politics.

A useful rule of thumb is to suspect all theological pronouncements made by politicians or other officials who require press agents, publicity managers, or advertising agencies to shape their image. Claims that we alone are protecting the flame, incarnating the purpose of history, must be seen as propaganda masquerading as theology, as atheism covering itself in false piety.

Because we are creatures of locality, nations will continue to envelop our beings and command our loves. But we should not confuse what is familiar with what is sacred. By denying ourselves the status of God's chosen people, we will force ourselves to relate to other nations as fellow "sinners," to use an old-fashioned word. Nothing is more dangerous than a world made up of warring holy lands. Much safer an international community of self-conscious paranoid nations. We might take our model for international community from Alcoholics Anonymous. The only "cured" alcoholics are those who remember day by day that they are alcoholics and refrain from drinking. The only safe nations are those who systematically innoculate themselves by a free press and a vocal prophetic minority against the intoxication of "divine destinies" and sanctified paranoia.

There is no hope for forming a transnational community, nor for the revival of authentic theology unless we see that war in its many forms is *the* major issue of our time. A theology that does not focus on the problem of creating an alternative to *Homo hostilis*, of discovering a historical alternative to replace the warfare state, is an idol of the tribe.

Perhaps the "death of God" or the disappearance of God we have heard so much about since the time of Nietzsche and Dostoevski is the sacred silence that will only be broken when we learn to hear the thundering small voice of individual conscience calling to us to shoulder the guilt and responsibility for our kingdoms of carnage. We cannot discover or await a revelation of

173

the true transcendence until we have given up the illusory comforts of false transcendence.

The second no is to the warfare against nature. Our existence is threatened equally by the warfare between nations and the war against nature, the immanence of man-made apocalypse, that comes with a bang or a whimper, nuclear suicide or technological ecocide. Therefore, we must withhold divine sanction from both *Homo hostilis* and *Homo faber*.

Warfare and the triumphant march of mindless technology are the twin demonic powers that currently are raging out of control and threatening to destroy the commonwealth we share with other forms of life. And so long as the "defense" budgets of the United States and the U.S.S.R. exceed the entire governmental budgets of the underdeveloped nations, and the least developed nations outspend the great powers in the proportion of their national budgets devoted to military hardware, the arms race and industrial pollution of the environment will go hand in hand. In our state of perpetual paranoid emergency, we spend our resources to defend ourselves against the enemy and cannot afford the luxury of curtailing any industry just because it happens to be polluting airsheds and poisoning ground water. Just as we can no longer find the sacred meaning of our lives in holy war, we can no longer base our dignity as humans on dominating nature. The identity we have forged by being *against*, and the God who has sanctioned our aggression, have brought us to the brink of self-destruction. Nationalism and species chauvinism are ideas whose time is past.

Paradoxically, the possibility of nuclear cosmocide and technological ecocide points clearly to an alternative to the dying God of War and Progress, to a new transcendent destiny, to the foundation needed for building a transnational community and a metanational immortality project. The transcendent destiny we require to inform our lives is as close as the ground we are standing on. The single sacred primal certainty on which we may build is "The earth is the Lord's, and the fullness thereof, and all they that dwell therein."

In spite of the spasmodic revivals of different forms of fundamentalism and nationalism, we live in a time of the death of God. We do not know an authentic trustworthy God to whom we may dedicate ourselves. And yet the question remains: "To what may we surrender?" The unsurrendered life is not worth living. Inevitably we must find something beyond our vulnerable

The Third World War has begun. It is the war against the earth.
Raymond Dasmann

Only if we regain contact with the source of our being in that nature within and about us will we be able to discover new road markers on the path ahead for the remainder of the century.
Glenn Gray

Apocalypse, with a bang or a whimper?

flesh in which to invest our hope. To date the twentieth century is strewn with the corpses of false faiths. The masses have surrendered to demonic gods. Perhaps the only surrender we can now make with full heads and hearts is to the "God beyond God," the metanational One who is calling us to reverence flesh and matter and create what has not been before—*Homo amicus.*

Certainly the task of envisioning, and creating a new psyche and a new polis should be sufficiently challeng-

rettet den Wald
sauvez la forêt
salvate il bosco
salvai il god
save our woods

Hans Erni. Switzerland
By personal permission

"I knew there'd be a catch in it when they said the meek would inherit the earth.
John Fischetti 1972 © News Group Chicago, Inc. 1986
with permission of the Chicago Sun Times.

ing to give us a new form of heroism and an immortality project to which we could dedicate ourselves with enthusiasm. The best energies of generations will be required for this new human vocation. The fateful vow "To duty," to "My country right or wrong" (which has been invoked in defense of genocide from Eichmann to Calley), must be replaced by the ancient Buddhist vow: "I vow to save all sentient beings." Needless to say, we will fail our vows time and again. We will make a million mistakes trying to invent the social institutions necessary to replace those that have given birth to and sustained the habit of war. The kingdom of AMOR will require more creativity and radical commitment than the empire of ROMA. We have been so conditioned by the politics of power that we do not yet know how even to imagine, much less implement, a politics of compassion. But we dare not dismiss the goal as utopian or impossible. Nothing could be more naive than to suppose that we can continue to extrapolate the hostility and the rapacious use of resources and political intransigence that is now "normal" and survive.

There is a single secure, sacred vocation to which human beings can surrender without the fear of falling into idolatry. *We are called to bring justice and compassion into the communal life of our species.* Our purpose is to create an order that is not red in tooth and claw, a commonwealth that is governed by our highest

ON THE THRESHOLD!

Gale. Los Angeles Times, 1920

capacity for consciousness, conscience, and compassion, rather than by our lowest capacity for inventing the means for the triumph of raw power. Precisely because the "objective" world does not incarnate the virtues of repentance and mercy, it is the human calling to do so. Ours is the task to so reduce the unnecessary "surplus" evil, that we will be left with the necessity of coping only with the inevitable evil of disease, tragedy, and death.

At present we possess neither a blueprint of utopia composed of a compassionate community of nations, nor a program for transforming the social and political institutions of *Homo hostilis*. Our new beginning must come from the acknowledgment that we have come to the end of the old. The proper stance for us is commit-

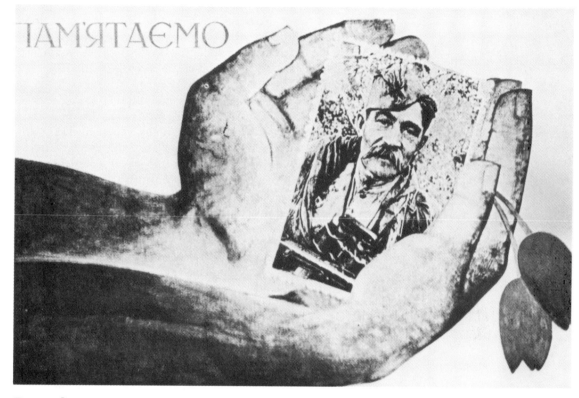

Remember
U.S.S.R.

ment to the discipline of questioning. If we don't yet know new answers, we can at least refuse to be hypnotized by old questions. Our addiction to the old question "How can we defeat the enemy and be secure?" is moribund. The question that must become an ultimate concern in our time is "How may we reduce our enmity?"

It is easy to despair when we stare at the dehumanizing images we create of the enemy and acknowledge how ingrained the habit of war has become in our species. But it would be dangerously wrong to draw the

I told you what my lies are. You have to tell me what your lies are.

Jessamyn Lovett-Keen, age 5½

conclusion of hopelessness. In a strange way the virulence and persistence of the archetypal images of the enemy are a hidden evidence of the ground of hope. We continually visualize our enemies in a demeaning way precisely because we are *not* instinctually sadists. If anything, we have a natural inclination not to kill our own kind, and therefore we have to make them horribly unlike us before we can overcome our instinctual compassion and can kill them. *Homo hostilis* must be created by the media and the institutions that subject him to a constant indoctrination by way of hero stories, ideology, rationalizations, tribal myths, rites of passage, and icons of the enemy. The entire institutional and symbolic apparatus of a society is necessary to maintain consensual paranoia and create a psyche that is governed by opposition to the enemy.

And even so the effort is successful only for a small minority. In spite of our best propaganda, few men and practically no women, will actually kill an enemy. In a remarkable study reported by Gen. S. L. A. Marshall in *Men Against Fire*, Army psychologists discovered that in combat conditions during World War II, the percentage of American soldiers who fired their rifle at a seen enemy even once did not rise above 25 percent, and the more usual figure was 15 percent. An amazing finding! Between 75 and 80 percent of trained combat troops will *not* willingly kill an enemy. General Marshall concluded from this study that, while the Army had dealt with men's fear of dying in battle, they had never dealt adequately with their reluctance to kill.

If it is so difficult to mold us into killers, we may yet turn our educational efforts to the more hopeful heroic task of doing battle with our own enmity. The mystical tradition in religion and its secular equivalent in psychotherapy has always tried to turn warfare inside out, to convert the extroverted aggression of the warrior into the introverted task of destroying the inner Pentagon — the defense mechanisms that isolate and make us hostile toward others. The true holy war is the struggle against the antagonistic mind.

PART 4

MEANTIME

Compassionate Warriors, Humane Enemies, and Tragic Battles

Evil is the rock on which all systems shipwreck.

Karl Jaspers

I am under no illusion that I have dissolved the mystery of evil. When we have repented of our paranoia, reowned the inhumane faces we have projected onto the enemy, and understood the psychology of enmity, there remain evils with which we must not compromise and enemies we must fight. While we Americans must acknowledge how wrong of head and hard of heart we

Nicaraguan (Sandinista?) Child. 1984

Guns or Children?
Helioflores. El Universal. Mexico
© 1985 by Cartoonists and Writers Syndicate

were in Vietnam (a mistake we are currently repeating in Nicaragua), we dare not minimize the suffering the Soviets are manufacturing in Afghanistan, or the Chinese in Tibet. Short of utopia there are real enemies. It is a luxury of the naive and sheltered to think that right thinking, good intentions, and better communication techniques will turn all enemies into friends. Even when we have thoroughly digested the systemic view of war, there remains a significant difference in degrees of guilt. And while we must learn to practice the rare virtue of metanoia, we must not assume that will allow us to adopt a pacifist position and refuse all responsibility for the use of military power. Quite possibly it would have been far more moral, in spite of the immorality of our war against Vietnam, to have continued to maintain an effective military presence in the area and to have intervened in Cambodia to prevent the genocide of the Pol Pot regime. Without question the poor and disenfranchised in Nicaragua had a real enemy in the person of Samoza, against whom pacifist sentiments and tactics were of no use. If freedom is the basis of all other human values, then there are times when men and women will have to choose between killing and surrendering their humanity.

The effort to understand the archetypes of the hostile imagination and the psychology of enmity can protect us from a host of illusions and can safeguard us against grievous mistakes. It can save us from dehumanizing ourselves by dehumanizing our enemies. It cannot save us from the agonizing dilemma of the systematic use of armed force. We must peel away layers of illusion, lies,

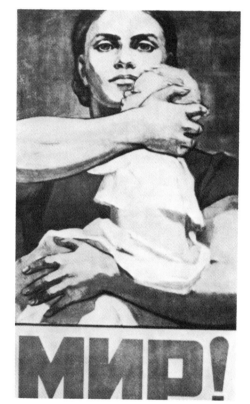

MNP means both "world" and "peace" in Russian.

Q. and A. from trial of Lt. Calley.
Peter Brandt, R. Haeberle. Museum of Modern Art. 1970

propaganda, projection but we are still left with the tragedy of violence.

Our best hope for remaining human, and remaining alive for the generations it will require to convert our disposition toward hostility to a disposition toward kindness, is to devote the full energy of our imagination and will to finding a way to live in relative harmony with our neighbors. For the time being, it is good enough if we can manage to avoid unnecessary battles and to place limits on the weapons with which we keep each other hostage to terror. And when we must fight, it must not be as holy warriors but as deeply repentant men and women who are caught in the tragic conflicts of a history that we have not yet had the vision, the will, or the courage to change.

And perhaps the great day will come when a people, distinguished by wars and victories and by the highest development of a military order and intelligence, and accustomed to make the heaviest sacrifice for these things, will explain of its own free will, "we break the sword," and will smash its military establishment down to its lowest foundations. Rendering oneself unarmed when one has been the best armed, out of a height of feeling—that is the means to real peace, which must always rest upon a peace of mind; whereas the so-called armed peace, as it now exists in all countries, is the absence of peace of mind. One trusts neither oneself nor one's neighbors, and, half from hatred, half from fear, does not lay down arms. Rather perish than hate and fear, and twice rather perish than make oneself hated and feared—this must someday become the highest maxim for every single commonwealth too.

Friedrich Nietzsche[32]

PART 5

POSTSCRIPT THE EDUCATION OF *HOMO AMICUS*

A Curriculum for Compassion

The education of *Homo hostilis*

You've got to be taught
To hate and to fear.
You've got to be taught
From year to year . . .

Italian Fascist boys organization, W.W.II.

Since the process of education for paranoia and warfare requires a total social effort, we must assume that the effort to create a compassionate psyche and society will require a similar or greater effort.

For instance, consider the massive reordering of economic priorities, gender definition, and family structure we would need to implement one of the fundamental changes necessary to create a gentle commonwealth. Psychological and cross-cultural studies make it clear that a society's propensity for gentleness and compassion is in direct proportion to the amount of touch, sensuality, esthetic appreciation, and caring sexuality that it encourages. Touch nurtures kindness. Lack of touch, harsh discipline, and ascetic rejection of sensory pleasures breeds violence. If we were to make the rearing of a gentle people an ultimate concern, the art of fathering and mothering and creating hearth might become the center of a new definition of heroism. An economic order focused on creating familiarity and community rather than profit could only be built by a "transvaluation of value," a radical switch from competition to cooperation. As unlikely (although necessary) as this seems at the moment, the proposal has a touch of irony, insofar as the original meaning of "economy" referred to the art of managing a household or a community and not the production, sale, and consumption of commodities. To nurture *Homo amicus*, we would have to cease conducting business on the model of warfare and make people more important than profit. Corporations, educational institutions, and governments alike would have to pay attention to creating an aesthetically delightful and personally nourishing environment within the workplace, the home, and the community.

As a summary of what we would need to know and do to create compassionate equivalents for war and as a way of beginning to imagine a process by which we might change our institutions and our psyches, I propose a social curriculum. This curriculum does not offer answers so much as it suggests the questions we should focus on and the kinds of knowledge and skills we would need to wean ourselves away from the habit of war. Which institutions will take seriously the problem of the nurturance of consciousness, conscience, compassion, and community, I do not know. Churches, schools, colleges, research institutes, the peace movement, should provide the leadership in implementing such a curriculum and restructuring our formal and informal educational system to make it reflect the priori-

. . . You've got to be taught
Before it's too late
Before you are six
Or seven or eight
To hate all the people
Your relatives hate.
from the musical *South Pacific*

Italian Fascist girls organization, W.W.II.

ties of survival rather than serving the conservative needs of preserving the status quo. In time, perhaps, the media, business, and last of all, government, may come to the aid of the species.

The following is a proposal in its infancy of some areas of knowledge, skills, questions, that will need to become widespread if we are to create a nonviolent community of nations.

The History of Warfare. Insofar as war is one of our most abiding social inventions, it should be studied in detail. Types of war: ritual, political, heroic, total. The political, economic, erotic, aesthetic, religious aspects of war. How is the warrior psyche created and sustained? How does the habit of war shape social institutions—the family, the relationships between the sexes, the church, government? The National War College might spearhead such studies.

The History of Peace. Under what conditions has peace broken out? What is necessary to sustain a cooperative relationship between persons, tribes, nations? What accounts for tribes such as the Hopi, Tasaday, Pygmies that have no mythology or practice of war? What are the social tradeoffs? How is the psyche and the institutional structure of peaceful peoples different from warrior societies? A National Peace Academy, jointly funded and housed with the National War College, might stimulate serious peace studies.

Paranoia and Propaganda. How does the consensual paranoia of a group shape its perceptions? How and for what reasons is the enemy created? What are the masks the enemy inevitably is made to wear in the war game? How do different types of societies convince themselves of the righteousness of their own national self-interest and the evil of the enemy's intention? How do the techniques of persuasions and molding public opinion to support war differ in media-rich and media-poor societies? How do propaganda styles differ in totalitarian and democratic countries? How do we determine the difference between our paranoid fears and real dangers? Which enemies do we manufacture out of our need for a scapegoat and which represent real threats that must be resisted?

Metanoia and Communication. How do we change our minds, see ourselves as others see us, reverse perspectives? How do we walk out the back door of our own minds, escape the prison of our ethnocentricity? What perceptual skills are necessary for us to see the familiar as strange and the strange as familiar? How do

185

Catholic education. Derry
© 1972 by John Giannini

we get the courage to admit our mistakes as individuals? How can nations ritually confess and atone for their corporate guilt in genocide and carnage? What kinds of families and institutions are necessary to create open, generous, and welcoming minds and personalities? How do we compensate for and protect others against our own inclination toward consensual paranoia?

Authority and Individual Conscience. How is conscience created? What are the stages of moral development? What obligations does an individual have beyond obedience? Duty? The Nuremberg Trials and the idea of crimes against humanity. Moral and transmoral conscience. The Milgram experiments. The authoritarian personality. Demystifying authority. The problem of authority and hyperdependence. When and how to defy authority. The obligation to resist wrongful authority. Heroes of conscience. How are men and women of exceptional conscience able to resist the institutions, bureaucracies, and authorities that sanction evil?

The Nature and Uses of Power. Types of power: rational, bureaucratic, charismatic, technical, moral, sexual, economic, religious. Violent and gentle forms of power. The relationship between power and impotence. The limits of the metaphor of power. Power and love.

186

Protestant education. Ulster
© 1972 by John Giannini

Army Junior ROTC.
It's an
education in itself.

Army Junior ROTC

Power, potentiality, and promise. Power as the genetic and social information that moves us toward the fulfillment of our potential. Are power and love antithetical? What are the relationships among love, power, and justice? Power as obsession and addiction. Power as the ability to empower others.

The Origins and Nature of Violence. Are we instinctually aggressive, violent, territorial animals programmed by selfish genes. Or do we learn to be violent? Harlow's deprived monkeys. Does lack of touch, sensory stimulation, maternal and paternal affection create violent persons and societies? A history of the routine cruelty inflicted on children in the name of discipline and molding. How much does the tide of violence recede when a society encourages touch, sensuality, caring sexuality? Eros and thanatos. Pleasure anxiety and peace phobia; why do we manufacture so much suffering and disease and avoid pleasure and health? Is violence an addiction?

Myths, Meanings, and Rituals of Compassion. How do we create an alternative to the warrior myth, the ritual of warfare, the battle (or military service) as rite of passage for males? What types of institutions are necessary to create and sustain *Homo amicus*? What new models for manhood can replace the heroic warrior? What ordeals, risks, adventures, challenges are involved in following the path of compassion rather than the path of power? Are there heroic lovers? What struggles, what risks would an individual, a community, a nation have to engage in to move from an orientation of power to a disposition of compassion? Is the concept of politics of compassion a contradiction in terms? Utopian? Too risky to contemplate?

Techniques for Social Change. The art of exerting

political pressure. Types of public power. Organization of voluntary associations. Empowerment of silent minorities and majorities. The formation of public opinion. The formation of metanational identities and loyalties. How may we love our country and justice? What types of education, experience, and institutions do we need to wean ourselves from the excesses of nationalism? International Peace Corps. Alternatives to military service in national armies. Might a first step in establishing the right to individual conscience be a multinational agreement to allow conscientious objectors to national wars to serve in international peace-keeping forces?

Conflict Resolution and Peace-making Skills. What skills are necessary to resolve conflict within the self, between individuals, in organizations, between nations? The art of negotiation and mediation. How do you find workable agreements with persons and nations more closed, hostile, and paranoid then you? The use of unilateral initiatives. How to change an enemy's policy without the use of violence. The place of threat and promise in negotiation. Creative listening. Discovering common ground. Understanding your opponent. Living with disagreeable differences. Tactics of persuasion in personal, institutional and national relations. Alternatives to conflict. Disarming aggression. The martial arts—judo, aikido, tai chi—as models. Going with resistance. Yielding to win.

Loving Combat. How do we exercise our love for competition and combat in nonhostile ways? Dialogue as loving combat. Games, Olympic and other, as peace-

Child's picture. El Salvador
"The soldier makes the peasant suffer and pursues the peasant people and wants to kill them."
© Matthew Naythons

Child's play. Cambodia
© 1973 by John Giannini

I would no more teach children military training than teach them arson, robbery or assassination

Eugene V. Debs

PEACE PLEDGE UNION

Peace Pledge Union

ful warfare. How can aggression be honored without encouraging violence? How may we deal with our enemies in a humane way? How is warfare limited? Made civil? Is there a possibility of returning the ideas of game, chivalry, and honor to warfare?

Empathy, Imagination, Compassion. What types of child-rearing practices create the most imaginative, empathetic, and compassionate adults? Where should the therapy aimed at repairing emotional dis-ease take place? Can and should schools teach us to be kind as well as smart? What increases our E.Q.—Empathetic Quotient?

Creative Excess and Dionysian Festivals. How do we provide for the need to break out of routine, escape the boredom of everyday life, to be purged by excess? Short of violence and war, how may we undergo these rituals of death and rebirth that we seem to need periodically as individuals and societies? What forms of ego transcendence should we encourage? Where are the dionysian skills, the art of surrender learned? What are socially responsible ways of dealing with our uncivil impulses toward cruelty and barbarous destruction?

Leadership and the Paradox of Power. How do we lessen the power-politics game when world leadership is mostly composed of men who are obsessed by power? What kind of changes would we need to choose our leaders from among the most psychologically healthy and wise segment of our population? How do we maximize the impulse to serve and minimize the need to accumulate power? Where is public conscience formed?

The Economics of Peace. How can we afford to demilitarize society? What might replace the arms industry? When profit, privilege, and ideology tend to be closely linked how is it possible to convert the military-industrial complex of the major arms-producing and -exporting powers to the creation of peacetime economies?

The Enemy Within. How do we create psychonauts, explorers of the heights and depths of the psyche? How do we dramatize the warrior of the inner battle who struggles against paranoia, illusions, self-indulgence, infantile guilt and shame, sloth, cruelty, hostility, fear, blame, meaninglessness? How does a society recognize and celebrate the courage of those who struggle against the demonic temptations of the self, who undertake a holy war against all that is evil, distorted, perverse, injurious within the self?

NOTES

1. Sue Mansfield, *The Gestalts of War* (New York: Dial Press, 1982).

2. Geoffrey Gorer, "Man Has No Killer Instinct," in Ashley Montagu, ed., *Man and Aggression* (London: Oxford Univ. Press, 1968), p. 34.

3. Ashley Montagu, "The New Litany of Innate Depravity," in *Man and Aggression*, p. 15.

4. *Christian Science Monitor,* 24 January 1983.

5. Laurens Van der Post, *Merry Christmas, Mr. Lawrence* (New York: Quill, 1983), p. 153.

6. Nevitt Sanford, *Sanctions for Evil* (San Francisco: Jossey-Bass, 1971), p. 164.

7. Robert Ivie, "Speaking 'Common Sense' About the Soviet Threat: Reagan's Political Stance," *Western Journal of Speech Communication* 48 (Winter 1984), pp. 39–50.

8. Farrel Corcoran: "The Bear in the Back Yard: Myth, Ideology, and Victimage Ritual in Soviet Funerals," *Communication Monographs* 50 (December 1983).

9. Central Intelligence Agency, FM 95-1A Guerrilla War Manual, 1984

10. *U.S. News & World Report,* 22 November 1982.

11. Konstantin Chernenko, as quoted in the *New York Times,* 13 June 1984, p. A-1.

12. Ronald Reagan, as quoted in the *New York Times,* 9 July 1985, p. A-12.

13. See Noam Chomsky, "Crimes by Victims Are Called Terrorism," *In These Times,* 24 July 1985, p. 17.

14. Press Reports on Soviet Affairs, 18 May 1984. Advanced International Studies Institute, Suite 1122 East-West Towers, 4330 East-West Highway, Washington, D.C. 20014.

15. Fred Schwartz, *You Can Trust the Communists (to Be Communists),* (Englewood Cliffs, N.J.: Prentice-Hall, 1960), p. 14.

16. J. Power, *Against Oblivion: Amnesty International's Fight for Human Rights* (Glasgow: Fontana, 1981), pp. 62–65.

17. Susan Griffin, "The Way of All Ideology," *Journal of Women in Culture and Society* 7 (1982), p. 3.

18. Mark Baker, *Nam* (New York: Berkley Books, 1983).

19. Gitta Sereny, *Into That Darkness* (New York: Vintage Books, 1983), p. 101.

20. J. Glenn Gray, *The Warriors* (New York: Harper & Row, 1970), p. 150.

21. Baker, *Nam,* p. 176.

22. S. L. A. Marshall, *Men Against Fire* (New York: Morrow, 1956), p. 39.

23. Otto Kroeger, personal conversation, 11 September 1985.

24. Robert Bathurst, "Two Languages of War," in Derek Leebaert, ed., *Soviet Military Thinking* (London: Allen & Unwin), p. 33.

25. Anthony Herbert, *Soldier* (New York: Dell, 1973), p. 402.
26. Robert Lifton, *Home from the War* (New York: Simon & Schuster, 1973), p. 353.
27. Headquarters, U.S. Army Training and Doctrinal Command, "Airland Battle 2000," p. 6.
28. Phillip Caputo, *A Rumor of War* (New York: Ballantine, 1978), p. 120.
29. Gilbert Herdt, *Guardians of the Flute* (New York: McGraw-Hill, 1981), p. 160.
30. William Broyles, Jr., "Why Men Love War," *Esquire* (November 1984).
31. William James, "The Moral Equivalent of War," in Staughton Lynd, ed., *Nonviolence in America* (Indianapolis: Bobbs-Merrill, 1966), p. 147.
32. Gray, *The Warriors,* p. 225.

SELECTED BIBLIOGRAPHY

Of the hundreds of books and articles I read in making this study the following I found most useful. Complete bibliographies appear in Falk and Kim (1980) and Woito (1982).

BOOKS

Arendt, Hannah. *Eichmann in Jerusalem.* New York: Penguin, 1963.

Becker, Ernest. *Escape from Evil.* New York: Free Press, 1975.
   See also my conversation with Becker, *Psychology Today,* April 1974. Becker has done monumental work on social structures by which we create surplus evil.

Brown, N. O. *Love's Body.* New York: Random House, 1966.
   Shows how the inner warfare is built into the structure of the Western personality.

Camus, Albert. *Neither Victims nor Executioners.* New York: Continuum, 1980.
   Eloquent plea for reason, clarity, and the necessity of utopian thought about ending war.

Clausewitz, Carl. *On War.* New York: Penguin Books, 1968.
   The old classic. Currently in high favor in both U.S. and U.S.S.R. military academies.

DeMause, Lloyd. *Foundations of Psychohistory.* New York: Creative Roots, 1982.
   Important work on the connection between abusive modes of child rearing and the habit of violence.

DeRougemont, Denis. *Love in the Western World.* New York: Harper & Row, 1974.

Makes some surprising connections between eros and thanatos.

Ellul, Jacques. *Propaganda.* New York: Vintage Books, 1973.
The best analysis of the way propaganda functions in contemporary societies.

Falk, Richard, and Samuel Kim. *The War System: An Interdisciplinary Approach.* Boulder, Colo.: Westview Press, 1980.
Overview. Good place to start for academic contributions.

Gray, J. Glenn. *The Warriors.* New York: Harper & Row, 1970.
The single most insightful account of men in battle yet written.

Griffin, Susan. *Pornography and Silence.* New York: Harper & Row, 1981.
Shows the sadomasochistic structure of "normal" society.

Herdt, Gilbert. *Guardians of the Flutes.* New York: McGraw-Hill, 1981.
Traces the development of the masculine personality in one particularly warlike society.

Keegan, John. *The Face of Battle.* New York: Penguin Books.
A reconstruction of the actual experiences of men in battle in different historical periods.

Lifton, Robert Jay. *Home from the War.* New York: Simon and Schuster, 1973.
The inner world of the American warriors in Vietnam and their enemy and the dehumanization of both.

Mansfield, Sue. *The Gestalts of War.* New York: Dial Press, 1982.
An inquiry into the origins and meanings of war as a social institution. Unique in offering a woman's perspective.

Marshall, S. L. A. *Men Against Fire.* New York: Morrow, 1967.
A report on the psychological difficulties the U.S. Army encounters in training men to kill.

Montague, Ashley, ed. *Man and Aggression.* London: Oxford University Press, 1968.
A review of the evidence that suggests we have no killer instinct, no genes for aggression.

Sanford, Nevitt. *Sanctions for Evil.* San Francisco: Jossey-Bass, 1971.
An important collection of essays exploring the ways in which society constructs a system for sanctioning killing, genocide, evil.

Tuan, Yi-Fu. *Landscapes of Fear.* New York: Pantheon Books, 1979.
A natural history and phenomenology of fear.

Walzer, Michael. *Just and Unjust Wars.* New York: Harper & Row, 1977.

Examines the moral issues involved in various aspects of warfare. Tightly argued, with historical illustrations as cases in point.

White, Ralph. *Nobody Wanted War.* New York: Doubleday Anchor, 1970.

A study of misperceptions in Vietnam and other wars.

Woito, Robert. *To End War.* New York: The Pilgrim Press, 1982.

One of the most comprehensive treatments of the complex changes we would have to undertake to create a world without war. Hopeful without being starry-eyed. The best bibliography I know on the politics of war.

ARTICLES

Griffin, Susan. "The Way of All Ideology." *Journal of Women in Culture and Society,* 1982, 7.

Ivie, Robert.

——. "Metaphor, Nuclear Arms, and the Reagan Re-election Campaign." Presented to Speech Communication Association Convention, 1984.

——. "Plainspeak and the Rhetorical Presidency: Literalizing Communist Savagery in Korea." Unpublished. Department of Communications, Washington State University, Pullman, Washington.

——. "Images of Savagery in American Justifications of War." *Communication Monographs* 47, November 1980.

——. "Speaking 'Common Sense' About the Soviet Threat: Reagan's Rhetorical Stance." *Western Journal of Speech Communication* 48, Winter 1984.

Professor Ivie's explorations of the decivilizing rhetoric used in American political speech parallels my explorations of the visual metaphors of the faces of the enemy. Thanks to him for sharing unpublished papers.

Kull, Steven. "Nuclear Nonsense." *Foreign Policy 5,* Spring 1985, p. 28–52.

A tightly reasoned analysis of perception theory and the type of nonsensical policies that follow from trying to stage-manage Soviet "perceptions" of the United States.

Rubinoff, Lionel. "*In Nomine Diaboli:* The Voices of Evil." In Israel Charny, *Strategies Against Violence.* Westview Press, Boulder, Colo.: 1978.

Shows how evil and violence have been perpetuated, institutionalized, and integrated into the bureaucratic duty of normal people. Could be called a study of the Devil in the Gray Flannel Suit.

Press Reports on Soviet Affairs.

A sampling of themes and issues currently in the Soviet Press. Available free from Advanced International Studies Institute, Suite 1122 East-West Towers, 4330 East-West Highway, Washington, D.C. 20014.

SOURCES OF IMAGES

A brief reflection on the type of images used and not used in this book will reveal a great deal about different styles of propaganda. The political poster with its brilliant graphics is the most successful propaganda tool in a media-poor society where it may be treasured as much for the splash of color it adds to a bare wall as for its political message. In media-rich societies the most effective propaganda is found less in any dramatic image of the enemy than in the suble way in which the "news" is chosen and presented in newspapers and television. Authoritarian societies organize propaganda from the top down and specialize in repeating stereotyped images, *ad nauseum*. In the U.S.S.R, for instance, the same three men have drawn a majority of the political cartoon posters for the last forty years. In so-called open societies propaganda springs spontaneously out of an unconscious consensus that remains uncritical of the ideology and policy of the majority and is reflected in editorial bias, cartoons, and entertainment media (Sylvester Stallone refused permission to use stills from his propaganda films *Rambo* and *Rocky IV*). In every society the true agents of freedom are the rare ones—the shaman, prophets, statesmen, and visionary cartoonists who see beyond the horizon of propaganda, demystify the image of the enemy, and direct our attention to our own complicity in the creation of injustice, war, and surplus evil.

There are several casual if not haphazard collections of unclassified propaganda but nothing that specifically examines the way in which the enemy has been perceived. The most useful method I found was to go into the war section of large libraries and pull all the oversized books off the shelves, on the theory that the photographs and images were most likely to be published in larger books. By this method I was able to glean many images that were not included in any of the standard collection of propaganda art.

LIBRARIES

Library of Congress, The Yanker Collection, Washington, D.C.

Hoover Library, Stanford University, Stanford, California. A large, but mostly unavailable collection of posters.

New York Public Library Picture Collection. Excellent collection of cartoons and propaganda art at your fingertips.

University of Michigan, Ann Arbor.

Mill Valley Library, Mill Valley, California. A marvelous cartoon collection in my back yard.

Presidio Army Museum, San Francisco.

Mitchell Wolfson, Jr., Collection of Decorative and Propaganda Arts. Miami-Dade Community College. Thanks especially to Stephan Greengard, Curator.

BOOKS

Editors of The Foreign Policy Association. *A Cartoon History of United States Foreign Policy 1776–1976.* New York: Morrow, 1975.

Robinson, Jerry. *The 1970s. Best Political Cartoons of the Decade.* New York: McGraw-Hill, 1981.

Hoff, Syd. *Editorial and Political Cartooning.* New York: Stravon Educational Press, 1976.

Darracott, Joseph. *The First World War in Posters.* New York: Dover, 1974.

Yanker, Gary. *Prop Art.* New York: Darien House, 1972.

Bild als Waffe. Mittel und Motive der Karikatur in funf Jahrhuderten. München: Prestel-Verlag, 1984.

INDIVIDUALS

Robert Weeks, for *Klatterdatsch,* the German magazine.

Jacques Leslie, for the Cambodian Buddha.

Jean Maggrett, for the akido drawings.

Jeanette Stobbie, for the us versus them, male-female stereotypes.

Lenny Lind and Joe Czop for additional photography.

Joel Spiewak, for contributing the use of his photographic studio.

The Esalen Soviet-American Exchange Project sent me to the U.S.S.R., where I was able to collect Soviet political art and lecture on "Faces of the Enemy" to the Academy of Sciences and other organizations. Thanks especially to Michael Murphy, Dulce Murphy, and Jim Hickman.

The Common Sense Foundation sent me to Nicaragua where I collected Sandanista political posters and had the opportunity to compare how propaganda functions in media-rich and media-poor societies. Thanks to Adam Friedson.

I owe a debt of gratitude to the cartoonists and artists who granted permission for their works to be included in this book. Especially, I thank Jerry Robinson, creator of "Life with Robinson" and the founder of the Cartoonists and Writers Syndicate. He opened his cartoon files to me, helped me secure permissions to reprint cartoons, and generously gave all manner of help. Without him this book would have been poorer in breadth and depth.